*successful methods
for teaching
the slow learner*

successful methods
for teaching
the slow learner

Muriel Schoenbrun Karlin

and

Regina Berger

PARKER PUBLISHING COMPANY, INC.
WEST NYACK, N.Y.

dedication

We dedicate this book to our colleagues who remain in the classroom despite the ever increasing challenge and the sometimes discouraging variety of problems they encounter daily. This book is dedicated, too, to the children of every race, creed, color or financial standing whom they teach. May it serve to draw both teachers and children together in a deeper understanding and love for each other.

acknowledgments

There may be some who feel that a school system as large as that of New York City discourages creativity. Quite the reverse is true, and we would like to thank a number of people for their creative contributions to this book—and for being a constant source of inspiration to us. They include: Mr. Maurice Wollin, District Superintendent, District 30, Staten Island, N.Y.; Mrs. Helen Harris, Educational and Vocational Counselor, Public School 82, Manhattan; Mr. Norman H. Harris, Principal, Anning S. Prall Junior High School, Miss Rose Anopol, Principal, Edwin Markham Junior High School, Mr. Charles A. Finkensieper, Principal, Public School 22, Mrs. Mary Peck, Teacher, Public School 22—all in Staten Island, N.Y.; and Mr. Raymond Dresher, Principal, Public School 138, Bronx.

Mr. Joseph Berman, of Anning S. Prall Junior High School was our photographer, and Mrs. Mary Davies of Public School 39 (Staten Island) was most helpful in the preparation of the manuscript. Permission for use of the photographs was granted most generously by Assistant Superintendent Jerome Kovalcik, Board of Education, City of New York.

We are grateful to Dr. Leonard Karlin, for his active support and constructive criticism. He did much of the difficult work of proofreading, and offered many valuable suggestions, comments and additions to the material. Also, a note of thanks to Lisa Karlin for her poem "Brotherhood" and to Mr. Henry Karlin for his many hours of library research.

a word from the authors
about this book...

To use one of the phrases popular with the in generation, this book will tell it like it is. There are educators who have, for years, been reluctant to admit there are "slow learners," and others have used a variety of phrases to describe this group. We believe there is every valid reason to believe there are large numbers of pupils who could correctly be called slow learners, and we believe just as strongly they can be taught successfully. In many ways, they are among the most rewarding students to teach. With a combined total of more than 50 years of experience, we have taught and worked with children of varying abilities, in a variety of socio-economic areas, and with wide variation in ethnic backgrounds. This book will concentrate on those specific, practical techniques which have brought the greatest success. Our objective is to help you understand the slow learner's problems, assist you in developing realistic solutions—and most of all to help you uncover that hidden desire to learn, which is usually a good deal more intense than surface behavior indicates.

Successfully teaching the slow learner requires the use of methods and techniques that stress ingenuity and creativity, and stimulate the minds of youngsters who have not been previously awakened. Each child must be provided with work he will be able to accomplish. This book describes hundreds of ways you can reach the slow learner, whether he demonstrates an inability to recognize and comprehend words and sentences, shows a limited vocabulary, has difficulty with arithmetical computations, finds it difficult to do abstract thinking, is handicapped by a short attention span—or for other reasons, has little interest in absorbing the things you're trying to teach. By sparking his imagination and motivating him to participate actively, you will achieve progress in various problem areas. Lessons must be personalized, so the student is able to comprehend the reason for including a particular topic, and more important, the reason for his mastering it. The slow learner might be described as the student who will not usually catch the ball when you throw it—simply because he is not interested in doing so. It is our task to encourage him, through you, to play a more active role in the ball game—and enjoy more of the benefits that will surely result.

One of the greatest thrills of teaching is to see the glow of recognition on a child's face when he arrives at a successful conclusion, or looking at the expression on his face when he sees you are delighted with a particular bit of progress he has made. This, as all of us know, does not happen by accident. It happens as the result of careful, systematic planning and the sustained use of fully developed, productive teaching techniques.

All the methods described in this book have been tested in a great many classroom situations. A major objective is to describe the more important, basic needs of the children, and to illustrate ways you will be able to fulfill many of them through your relationships in the classroom and through the lessons you develop. This individual fulfillment is an absolute necessity if the slow learner is to change his previous pattern, and learn successfully.

Most of the techniques are adaptable to various levels of education. You will find they lend themselves to variation and, indeed, it is recommended you make such changes as will fit the particular requirements of the children in your classroom. For example, the same basic method may be used to teach vocabulary to a third grader, or to a student several grades higher. It is the approach we suggest to you—and your own refinements will make it even more applicable to your own class.

You will probably agree that enthusiasm and love of learning must be communicated to the slow learners. In addition, his self-image must be changed so that he is made to feel he *is* capable of learning. More importantly, so he feels an infinitely greater *desire* to learn. Because he has probably failed so often in the past, he now needs to experience academic success. He needs to comprehend the fact that the skills and knowledge you offer to him will have a direct bearing on his entire life. By applying the various methods included in this book, you can effectively assist him in this development and, in turn, you will discover each day's labors become more stimulating and more challenging to you as you multiply your success in teaching the slow learner.

contents

3. DISCIPLINE AND THE SLOW LEARNER: CONTROL-
LING YOUR PUPILS UNTIL THEY DEVELOP SELF-
CONTROL (*Continued*)

*work apply to their lives, as much as possible · Work to build
a success pattern · Produce plays wherein each pupil can
take part · Look for techniques which hold all the children's
interest, never forgetting the slow learner · Each child is a
part of the entire class and no one can be a law unto himself · Learn of your children's lives*

*Teaching to listen · Teaching children to speak · Writing ·
Teaching · Poetry · Illustrating poems · Background material · Writing verse · Writing a class poem · Making
"poetry pouches" · Teaching vocabulary through poetry ·
Games with poems · Poetry as a moral force*

*Building a success pattern · Motivating the reading skills
program · Recording the results · Teaching reading · Experience charts · Prepare your own reading materials · Review unfamiliar words taught during the week · Individualized reading · Class libraries · Teaching vocabulary in
language arts · Word wallets · Meet a new family of words
each week · Teaching children to love words · Teach one
new word a day · Building vocabulary in other subject
areas · Teaching reading skills in all subject areas · Duplicate your own materials · Using contextual clues to learn the
meanings of new words · Selection of the main idea of a
paragraph · Reading and thinking critically · Summarizing
any reading material · Reading and following printed directions · Readings for safety and for health! Interpreting signs
and labels · Using the parts of a book efficiently · For all
skills · Now! Let's get them to read*

1

recognizing the slow learner

In order to successfully teach slow learners, the teacher must relate to them on two levels—intellectually and emotionally. Paraphrasing this, we must teach both with our brains and our hearts. We must become so aware of certain aspects of the children's lives that these aspects in turn become part of *our* subconscious minds. As one aspect, let us consider the effects of poverty: Many children are slow learners as a result of financial or intellectual impoverishment, and poverty may cause physical or psychological handicaps that preclude learning. For example, the slow learner most often experiences difficulty in reading. This is directly related to his lack of the basic communication skills—speaking and listening. Many times these are sadly neglected in the homes of the poor, where children are often encouraged to be seen and not heard, or where they are chased from the house into the street early in the morning, and left there until late at night. The vocabulary development of these children may suffer as a result of the lack of communication with adults. It is difficult to believe, but there are native born children entering our schools whom we must, literally, teach to speak English, and to communicate.

Another aspect, which we often take for granted, is a lack of cultural background. A child whose home lacks books, magazines, and newspapers, must be introduced to printed pages. He may be meeting them for the first time in the classroom. His physical awareness extends, in a vast number of cases, only to his immediate environment. Often he has spent almost his entire life within a radius of four or five blocks. He has never been to a

1

museum, a zoo, or even a library. The slow learner often has no motivation to learn. He is required by law to attend school, but what law in the world is able to force him to take part in the learning process?

Our tasks are cut out for us. We must try to help this child to overcome his handicaps. We must help him to read, to eliminate feelings of discomfort when he is confronted by words, to build his experiential background and widen his horizons. Being aware of his needs, we can try to fulfill them—the need for love and affection, for a feeling of security, and for a sense of accomplishment. Methods, techniques and strategies will be outlined for you which will, in part, help you to accomplish this.

Remembering that the slow learner is an individual child with differences in needs and abilities, we suggest basic procedures you may wish to follow, or to modify; making sure his handicaps are not of physical origin; giving him more of your time and attention; showing him you are anxious to help him; placing him in a group of children who need instruction in similar skills; giving him status; handling him with patience if he suddenly stops learning (if he forms a mental "block"); getting him to produce good work and exhibiting it; motivating and guiding him so that he strives to eliminate his own handicaps, and develops an interest and a positive feeling toward the classroom and education.

We are administering to his intellectual needs when we teach him vocabulary and reading, mathematics and social studies. We are nourishing him emotionally when we show him love and affection, when we make him feel he belongs, when we establish situations in which he can achieve success and develop feelings of self-worth. Are they not equally important?

PROFILE OF THE SLOW LEARNER

A. He most often comes from a poverty stricken home

Many of our slow learners come from what our newspapers refer to as "culturally disadvantaged" homes. (This term is often used as a euphemism for "poor.") We find these youngsters in all groups; among the Negro and the white, the seventh generation American, and the immigrant. They may be children from Appalachia, Hong Kong, or from Main Street. But in most cases, these slow learners come from impoverished families.

The extent of poverty in our nation today is far greater than most of us realize. In New York City, there are more than 850,000 people being supported by the New York City Department of Social Services. They are so often apathetic and resigned to their present situation that they do not see the hope that education—and, regrettably, it is only education—can bring them! This is our first job—to inspire children, to convey to them the idea that they can rise above their environments, as many people before them have done. We must teach them that there is hope—that even today, trite as it may sound, America is still the fabled "land of opportunity." Our President has said no child need forego a college education for lack of funds. We must bring this home to each and every child—to show each one he can, if he will educate himself, make a higher place for himself in our society. But we cannot convey this idea if we do not believe it ourselves.

In regard to the actual physical effects of poverty, research biologists have announced a hypothesis which, if proven, may be a key to some of our problems. They have stated that if a pregnant woman eats a diet lacking in sufficient vitamins, her child may be born with poorer brain development, and therefore decreased intelligence. This is the direct link between poverty and slow learners. While the problem is being studied, physicians are prescribing vitamin pills for women during pregnancy, but far too many of our poor women do not see their doctors until they are in the sixth or seventh month of pregnancy—which is late, in terms of the formation of the embryonic brain.

There is another variety of poverty—although it is not economic. The child whose parents have no time for him—who are so busy with careers or with the golf course that he grows up alone, or with servants caring for him—is also impoverished. The "poor little rich girl" is not a mythical character; she does exist—surprisingly often. We know of many children from financially secure backgrounds who have become behavior problems in or outside of school as a result of this emotional deprivation. How often we read of such cases in our newspapers! Not one, but many celebrities, have "trouble" with their children because they have not taken the trouble to guide them.

We must consider each child as an individual; when he has problems, we must study them, always keeping his background in mind.

B. He is unable to communicate

Have you ever encountered, or has the thought crossed your mind that there are children who have not learned the very fundamental skill of speaking? When a family of nine is forced to live in one or two rooms, the children are encouraged, or pressured to keep quiet. They do not get the opportunity to use words or to learn their meanings. They may not hear English spoken. You must, in any grade, teach such children to express themselves in words, instead of gestures; statements instead of fists; sentences instead of screams. Of course, if a child does not have this knowledge of speech, how can he ever learn to read or write? Speaking is one of the most fundamental of the language arts skills, basic to the others. How does one teach a child to speak? It is a long, difficult process, but it starts with encouragement.

1. Allow him to feel free to speak.
2. Encourage him to do so.
3. Praise him when he does.
4. Set up situations in which he will speak:

   a. For example, tell the children a story or have them watch a film or a TV program, but stop it before it ends. Then have each child tell how he expects it to finish. Repetition is unimportant; what is important is getting the child to speak.

   b. You may wish to use a pair of telephones, sometimes available from your local telephone company, to foster speaking. If you cannot borrow these toy phones, even those made by connecting tin cans with cord can be just as valuable.

5. Stress vocabulary—the vocabulary the child should actually use in his daily life, and have him use these words in the work you do with him in class. For this experience, charts are particularly good. We will outline this technique in Chapter 5. The need for vocabulary improvement can be seen in this typical true story.

In one of the Operation Head Start schools a four year old was brought to the supervisor screaming. He screamed and he kicked, and kept shrieking, "You _____, you _____, you _____!" He had hurt his knee, and the Head Start teacher was attempting to clean it with peroxide. After the task was finally finished, the lady talked with the child.
"Didn't you know we were trying to help you?"
"Yep."
"Then why did you keep screaming?"
"It hurt."
"But why were you using such a bad word? You know you don't use words like that in school."
"But, teacher, I don't know no other word."

Vocabulary knowledge is one of the major parts of the test used to calculate the I.Q. (Intelligence Quotient). In many cities it has been discarded because it was considered to be invalid, after it was realized that while culturally deprived children may be deficient in this knowledge, they are not necessarily unintelligent. As teachers, our work is clear. We must increase our pupils' use of words, expand their powers of self-expression. This chapter is devoted to philosophy for the most part, and so there are only a relatively few methods and strategies contained herein. Subsequent ones will be more practical—giving you many specific skills, and then telling you how you may teach the slow learner successfully. Remember, too, that "words are the ambassadors of the soul!"

C. He lacks experiences

When youngsters are brought up in a limited, sterile or hostile environment, their intellectual and spiritual development is hindered or marred. They rarely experience new situations, or get any sort of intellectual stimulation in the home. As an example, we can point to children living on Staten Island, one of the five boroughs of New York City. Separated from Manhatten and all of its wonders by a ferryboat ride costing only 5 cents, these boys and girls have never, ever, visited the magic island across the bay! The converse is true of people living in Manhattan. Certainly the majority of them have never visited Staten Island, or seen the longest bridge in the world, the Verrazzano-Narrows, which connects it to Brooklyn. Yet Staten Island is part of New York City, and the seventh grade social studies curriculum includes it.

In order to help the culturally deprived children, we must supply intellectual stimulation, which acts as a catalyst in the learning process. What would a trip to Staten Island bring to the child from a typical urban environment? He would travel across New York Bay, coming quite close to Liberty Island, and its famous "grande dame." He would see some of the ocean-going traffic entering and leaving one of the world's greatest ports. On the Island itself, he could visit High Rock Park, a conservationist's dream, which still has virgin forests and lands unchanged since the time the Indians roamed through them. He might go to the Richmondtown Restoration and see a Dutch schoolhouse, with the residence of the teacher attached, called the Vorleezer House. All these experiences are readily available, but unfortunately, so rarely taken advantage of. Aren't there such places of interest in or near your area—zoos, libraries, radio or TV stations, banks, colleges, movies, plays, ballgames; visits to hotels, to department stores, to food distributors, to which some trips may be arranged?

Why should you, the teacher, bother to take children on trips and do other things to try to make up for this lack of experiences? Consider the following: Children who have spent much of their early lives in Puerto Rico often have difficulty learning to read the word "train." Upon investigation, it is discovered that they had never encountered such a vehicle! We must supply many and varied experiences for our reluctant learners, for our culturally deprived. Remember, that while a trip to a place nearby is not exciting for you, it may be very thrilling for a child who has never been more than three blocks away from home.

There are so many things we, as teachers, take for granted.

We have graduated from college, and so we have a familiarity with books of all sorts. They have become almost as great a part of our lives as food, shelter or clothing. Yet there are many homes where a book gains entry only when a child brings it from school. We have given children newspapers and magazines and been thanked profusely for them—because they are a rarity. It is very difficult for us to understand what culturally disadvantaged really means, because most of us have never experienced such extreme deprivation. Not only that, but rarely do we associate closely with those whose lives have been blighted by poverty and ignorance. We have visited homes where the only visible furniture was unmade beds and tables. In this situation, one hardly thinks of books. Yet, if we do not introduce them, and foster an interest in them, how will this intellectual wasteland ever end?

There is one source of stimulation which is a double-edged sword, but which we cannot possibly ignore. This is television. There is no doubt that youngsters learn from it. Have you seen a four year old pick a product from the shelves of a grocery because it is advertised so often on the programs he watches? There are television sets found in homes where a book is never opened, a newspaper never bought, a magazine non-existent. In rural England, one sees picturesque white cottages with thatched roofs, and television antennae extending above them.

Very often in September a teacher will ask his or her pupils to write a composition on, "What I Did Last Summer." For a child who went nowhere, and did nothing; or who certainly would not tell, voluntarily, about the stunts he pulled, or the time the police picked him up—what is there to say? But pupils like this have written compositions for us about rockets being launched, or races run at Indianapolis, because of the wonder of television. We are all aware of how much smaller the world has become, thanks to such miracles as Telstar. Television can be one of our tools, if we use it constructively. We cannot assume that all pupils have sets in their homes, but we can use them when they do. Perhaps the greatest objection to the medium is the amount of violence pictured on it, before our very eyes. This is not only true of fictional broadcasts, but also of real life. How many millions saw the shooting of Lee Harvey Oswald by Jack Ruby? This factor cannot be ignored, but it does not mean that we must

condemn the medium completely. We must learn to use it, and
teach our pupils to profit by it in a wholesome manner. Instead
of "What did you do last summer?", we suggest you try asking
your slow learners, "What is the most important event which
happened last summer—in your actual life, in the movies or on
television?"

D. He is often unaware
of his background and
heritage

"Mommy, where do I come from?" This was the very first time
the seven year old boy had asked his mother what could have
been a very embarrassing question. She, being very modern, pro-
ceeded to give the biological and physiological explanation. She
spoke sagely, and at length, about sperm and egg, womb and
birth. Before she finished, her son interrupted her. "No, no,
mommy. Jimmy Brown comes from the Bronx. Where do *I* come
from?"

Children do want to learn about their backgrounds, their her-
itage. However, we should not try to make them into miniature
adults. We must work at their level of understanding. The present
demands for the teaching of Negro history are, for example, very
well founded. All children need to have pride in themselves, in
their culture, and what it has contributed to civilization and to
our nation. White children, too, need to learn of the Negro's contribution to our national growth. This information should surely
be included in the history books we are using today.

We believe this continuity with the past should be studied and
stressed. John Kennedy, before becoming President of the United
States, wrote a short book called "A Nation of Immigrants." How
true this title is! Except for those of us who descended from the
American Indian, don't we all fall into that category? By presenting this concept to children, we uplift them—in their own
eyes. Certainly each wave of immigration has added to our wealth
of culture, and the Puerto Rican child, the Chinese, the Italian,
or the Polish, each should be made to feel the value of his an-
cestors' contribution. In our nation the role of the very early
immigrants has been given too much prestige.

One reason for the greatness of our country is its diversity of cultures. How boring—if we lost this, if we were all alike, if we cooked and spoke and thought alike. The child from a "different" background is often ashamed of it. He is often considered to be a slow learner, when what he really needs is acculturation. You can help him to turn the shame to pride, to see that "Where do I come from?" is very important—but more so is, "Where am I going?"

E. He lacks motivation

If one had to choose the most important concept in education, it would be, without question, motivation. Like the biblical David conquering Goliath, the power of a desire to accomplish something is tremendous. If we can motivate all of our slow learners to learn, we too can kill the giant, against the worst possible odds. Certainly, it is harder to motivate these children. As we have said, they are very special children, because they are handicapped. Their problems are often multiple in nature. They may be hostile or apathetic; they may be doing a minimum amount of work— just enough to get by—or they may be doing absolutely no work in school at all. But if we can motivate them, what a difference! We have seen pupils almost literally come alive when they "discover" electricity, or when they are introduced to Edgar Allan Poe. We have heard of a boy learning to read in six months, after six years of failure, because he wanted to construct a motor and had to read the plans for it himself. We know of children, considered to be slow learners, working long hours in the library to prepare debates for social studies. There are many ways to motivate your children, and we shall try to help you to develop your skill as a teacher so that you will be able to "hook them," to get them interested—to really motivate them.

F. He is unable to read

Most educators would agree that the primary difficulty of the slow learner is reading. Suffering from this, he falls into a pattern which very often damns all of his days in school. He may develop in different ways as a result of this: He may become hostile—and fight at the slightest provocation. He may become apathetic—and allow life in school, with all that is attendant upon it, to pass him by. He may even fall into a group which tries and sometimes manages to achieve a modicum of success, but all too often fails; and from this alternate acceptance and rejection, becomes frustrated. It is possible that he may even achieve enough success to fool himself into thinking that all is well, and seem perfectly content with his lot in life. In actuality, he is achieving little. All of these possibilities exist in our classrooms today.

SOME GENERAL CONSIDERATIONS FOR THE TEACHER

A. Respect for the individual

From the concept of pride in one's background, we move very quickly to the idea of respect for the individual. Each individual is precious to us.

Respect in the classroom applies to both the teacher and the students. You should respect them, and they, in turn, should respect you. This, too, is not as easy as it sounds. How can you respect children when they are dull or inattentive, screaming or giggling, shouting obscenities or physically violent with one another, or even with you? By your manner, however, you can handle many difficult situations, handle them well, and still treat the children with respect.

This story will illustrate.

A new and very distressed teacher came to his supervisor. He had been forced to take a girl out of his class because she had told him, point blank, "I will not behave in here!" The assistant principal questioned him. The teacher warned the class that anyone who did not behave and interfered with his teaching would be disciplined. To the teacher's surprise, the supervisor was obviously delighted. Then he explained, "The young lady you removed from class—I know her very well.

She usually would have replied with a profane expression. Can you see what progress you have made with her?" Because she had been treated with respect, the child had responded without the use of her usual vulgarity.

In dealing with children it has been said, "We teachers have to love them when they are least lovable." The best way to teach any concept, and particularly love, is by living it.

Many children use language which might make an adult blush. You must not be shocked; neither ignore it. You will find that children will react to you as an individual and, unless provoked, will not usually curse or swear at you. If they do, however, use a comment such as, "This is not the way we express ourselves here. Please stop! We don't speak to you that way, and we don't expect you to speak that way to us!"

If you honestly believe this, and you can accept the fact that some children regard you as a threat, and are reacting to you in this way although you personally are not, and if you are able to understand this, you are in a position to win them over. The biblical truth, "A soft voice turneth away wrath" is particularly effective in the classroom. It is so easy to magnify offenses, and create "incidents," as long as teachers allow themselves the expensive luxury of getting excited.

B. Supplying the basic needs of children

All children, and particularly our slow learners, need love and affection, a feeling of security, a sense of being wanted and a feeling of self-worth. Surely we know that the prime responsibility for fulfilling these needs lies in the hands of the parents, and just as surely we know that in some homes this is completely ignored. Many children get, instead of love and affection, blows and vituperation; instead of security, a feeling of being an adjunct, or a nuisance. They may come from broken homes, where there is not one father, but a succession of stepfathers, uncles and friends. They may come from homes where no one has any time for them.

Can you always recognize these children when you see them? Not usually—unless you talk to the child at length; even then, you may not learn anything because children are so sensitive, so ashamed of these things, that they will try to conceal them. You may never learn of the cruelties or tragedies in their backgrounds. Occasionally the teacher learns of these after the child has gotten into trouble in the school. The broken home so often breaks the child. The love he lacks manifests itself, so often, in the way he acts. When a child comes to school with a blackened eye or a battered head, try to ascertain the causes of the injuries. They may have been inflicted by a drunken father or a frustrated or rejected mother, or by some other member of the family who may possess a sadistic streak. The sympathy you feel for the child will awaken in him an affection for you, and possibly a desire to confide in you. Your tender feelings for him will be the first avenue of communication with this unfortunate child. A genuine smile, a warm word of encouragement, an interest in the child's life, a kindly pat on the shoulder might be a partial antidote for the cruelties he has suffered at home.

What else can you do? Can you even partially fulfill the need for love and affection which is so strong and so basic, and so often lacking in children's lives? Yes, you can. You may, in part, become the parent figure the child longs to have. You can make your classroom a place where children feel loved, where they feel comfortable. You cannot possibly substitute for a parent all of the time, but you may represent the mother or father who possesses kindness and understanding. Some teachers begin their careers feeling love for all children, but soon start hating some of them as a result of their own inadequacy in structuring the classroom situation. We will try to show you specific ways in which you can create a climate which will bring out the best in your pupils and in you. This occurs in a class where you have control; and where there is a feeling of security, respect and affection between teacher and children. Slow learners will achieve far more in such an environment. Boys and girls must not encounter the same chaos and disorder which many of them experience in their own homes. They need you to structure this situation and develop a climate in which they can learn and develop spiritually and intellectually.

C. The teacher must always act professionally

Are you easily provoked to anger? If you are, you will find this a decided handicap. Teachers must search their souls, and recognize their own fears. Very often adults are either afraid of the children, or of their own potential for violence. We have seen big men, terrified by their own impulses toward their students. This fear manifests itself in many ways; one of these is to provoke arguments.

How do you react when a child tells you, "No, I won't." If you get furious, you will have trouble, severe trouble. If you can say, "Please, I need your help," you are just too good to be true. Most of us fall somewhere in between, depending on the particular circumstances. But children, and particularly our slow learners, do say "No," and you simply must expect it and learn to tolerate it.

Many slow learners are highly volatile and very easily provoked. Many do not like—indeed cannot tolerate—being physically touched. We have heard it phrased, "Don't touch the merchandise." Have you ever felt a child recoil when you put your hand out to stop him from running? Be very careful about using your hands for any reason. Your strength must be in your voice, in your presence.

Learning what upsets your children, what gets them going, and then avoiding these situations is equivalent to throwing strikes in a ball game. You can, so often, avoid trouble—not allow it to develop—by having work for your class to do from the moment they enter your classroom until the time they leave it. Chaos is uncomfortable for most children, and they will help you to avoid it. Some will need constant reminders, but if your tone is a pleasant one ("Come on. Let's go. Let's get to work."), they will cooperate. Perhaps not every child, but many of the members of the class can be settled down this way. You can then direct your attention to those who are not. Some of them will respond to further gentle chiding. Inevitably there are one or two children, usually slow learners, who have no pencils, or pens, no notebooks or papers. It is simple enough to have a few of these items on hand, to lend to them. You must, however, insist that each child begin working promptly. If the assignment is interesting, you will find it far easier to get cooperation.

A bored child is not going to learn. He may be a slow learner or he may not, but if he is bored, the wall has gone up around his mind. Your job is to breach it. We will try to show you how. While it is true that one person's methods may not work for everyone, you will have bases from which you can work out your own variations.

D. Special treatment for the slow learner

Here are some general suggestions which may prove useful. They are applicable to children on any grade level, elementary or secondary.

1. Very often we are too quick to designate a child as a slow learner without considering the possibility of physical defects. Be sure to recommend to the parent that the vision and hearing of the child be checked if you find he is having learning difficulties. Poor reading frequently may be attributed to poor eyesight. Vision may change as the child grows, and suddenly a youngster may find his vision has deteriorated. If you deem it necessary, refer the child to the school nurse or doctor; if glasses, or a hearing aid, is needed, be sure the parent is informed, and that he obtains the help the child needs.

2. Give slow learners more time and attention than you do to the other children. The reason is elementary—they need it more. By being patient and encouraging the child, you help him to grow and develop without being scared psychologically. Show him you are anxious to help him, and get him to seek your help. If you wish to call him up to your desk when the class is working, motion to him, and ask him quietly, "Is there anything I can help you with, now?" It is possible that, with your help, some of his problem areas may disappear. Make him feel his questions are welcome.

3. Seat him closer to you and, if your class is heterogeneously organized, next to a bright child. Be sure, however, that they are

compatible. Structure the situation so that the slow learner is able to accept the help of the other child.

4. Form groups to teach new skills, or to strengthen those skills in which the children are deficient. You may wish to give a diagnostic test to the entire class in order to help you form these groups. By preparing this test carefully, you will be able to determine which children have needs in common, and then keep them together. Within the groups, you should have the children work independently, and at other times together. By varying the routine lessons you make your class far more interesting.

5. Whenever possible, give your slow learners monitorial jobs. They need to feel important and to develop self-confidence, particularly if they have had little academic success. Of course you should speak to them in the same tones you use to speak to the brighter children; never become annoyed by the inability to learn. These slower children should not feel different or handicapped.

6. If a child seems suddenly to be blocked in his ability to learn, he needs your patience and sympathetic understanding. Speak to him gently. Try to explain the work you are doing very carefully. Simplify the thought and the wording. If he still appears perplexed, change the subject, saying, "We will return to this some other time." Each of us knows of someone who "blocked out" a subject because he was ridiculed, or placed in a situation where he felt terribly inferior.

7. When the slow learner presents you with written work (Illustration 1-1) worthy of exhibiting, be sure that it is displayed. Encourage him to take part in plays and class discussions. Strive to build his self-esteem, so that he has poise and a feeling of self-worth.

8. Guide the handicapped child in working toward elimination of his problem areas. If he has an older brother or sister in the school, enlist the aid of the sibling. Make the slow learner aware of any resources the school has to assist him, such as tutorial programs, or coaching personnel.

Invite the child's parents to confer with you, and suggest ways in which they can help the child. Give concrete suggestions, not vague generalities. For example, you might tell a parent to have

Illustration 1-1

the child read aloud for ten minutes per day to gain reading fluency. The parent may then ask the child questions about the material he has read to get some idea of the youngster's comprehension. He may ask the child to select the main idea of the selection, or to define any new words encountered. Parents are often anxious to help their children, but simply do not know how. It is worth our time and effort to instruct them in these techniques.

SUMMARY

The slow learner is often from a poverty stricken home. Because of conditions within this home, he may be unable to communicate and lacking in even the fundamental skill of speaking. His word knowledge is sometimes pitifully meagre. Many slow learners have had few cultural experiences—they have rarely left the immediate neighborhood in which they have been born and brought up. Their school lives have not been satisfying, and they have lost the motivation for learning which may have been present when they were very young. One of their most significant characteristics: they usually are unable to recognize words and to comprehend much of the material they are reading.

As a teacher, you may have encountered only one or a few slow learners in a class, or you have had entire classes in which they are the rule rather than the exception. In any case, these boys and girls must be treated with respect, in order for them to be able to accept learning from you. They have basic needs which it is possible you may help them to fulfill. You must act professionally at all times.

There are certain techniques to utilize with all slow learners: Determine whether they have sight or hearing problems, which might make them appear to be slow. Give them more of your time and attention; while the class is engaged in work you have assigned, you may concentrate on helping them with their specific problems. Show them you are anxious to be of help—that you do not consider them to be pests or nuisances. Seat them close to you, so that in free moments they may ask questions of you. Form groups, to individualize your teaching. Occasionally make

Illustration 1-2

the slow learners monitors, so that they may gain in status—in their own eyes.

If a child seems to be "blocking," he needs a great deal of patient help. Simplify the work as much as you can, or temporarily leave the subject. Praise any work which is done well, and is truly praiseworthy, and exhibit it—again to build the child's self-esteem (Illustration 1-2). Give slow learners guidance, and motivate them to try to solve their problems—with your help, of course. Do not allow them to give up.

There is one overriding factor which will determine to a large extent your success or failure as a teacher of slow learners. Do you really love children? Do you care about them, about their development, their ultimate success or failure, their happiness as human beings? If you feel this love, then the compassion, interest and joy that you will get from seeing these youngsters grow and develop will tremendously enrich that part of your life which you devote to them.

2

developing daily and yearly lesson plans for the slow learner

Few of life's activities do not benefit from careful planning. Many are totally impossible without it. Teaching is one of these. In this chapter you will find included a brief discussion of the yearly lesson plan or calendar. All of the aspects of the daily lesson plan will be covered in detail; the aim, the motivation, the concepts you will cover, the pivotal questions you should ask, the type of homework assignment which you may choose to give, and the individualization you can do to meet the needs of each child. You will find, too, a description of the "warm-up," a part of the lesson extremely useful in the junior or senior high school. In making your plans, you must provide for the children in your class who are slow learners. The more interesting your topics and their presentation, the more likely you are to entice their attention.

One of the authors recalls with pleasure a school experience which took place while she was teaching in a poverty blighted area.

> She remembers with affection a pair of dark eyes that turned toward her as she stood in front of her classroom, telling the fifth grade children the story of Abraham Lincoln. She warmed to her subject as she saw the boy's gaze fixed upon her face. He had been labeled a "slow learner." Whatever his I.Q. might have been, judging from the look on his

19

face, the child was not emotionally impoverished. He listened, with rapt attention, to the story of the martyred President. At the end of the school day, she approached the child and told him, quite truthfully, how delighted she was to see, by his attention to the lesson, that the child shared her deep love for one of our greatest presidents. She offered him a book on the life of Abraham Lincoln, which he accepted eagerly. Not being a very good reader, the child told her that his mother could help him understand it. The teacher suggested that they read the book together. He consented enthusiastically. Then she asked him whether he would like to find some poem about Lincoln to read to the children at the next assembly meeting. "Oh, yes, oh yes!" answered the little boy fervently. As the teacher's hands reached up on the wall where she had tacked a picture of Abraham Lincoln, the child looked at her earnestly and said, "Can I have that picture, teacher?" With a deep sense of gratification, she handed it to him, thinking, "It was worth all the effort to find the picture and the book and bring them into school." This child, who was often so inattentive, so uninterested and rebellious, apparently had a tremendous power to love—to love a man he had never seen. For the first time, the teacher had caught glimpses of the child's emotional potentialities. "Perhaps it is I, and not the little boy, who is the slow learner," she thought. "Isn't it remarkable that a person dead almost a hundred years has brought this child closer to me?"

The success of this lesson arose from the teacher's careful planning of the story of Abraham Lincoln, with all of its noble detail, her finding the picture and just the right book which would appeal to young children, being ever mindful of keeping it within the range of their comprehension.

As we discuss planning, we should keep in mind the slow learner, for the wise teacher will realize that he must be able to allot more of his time and attention to this child; that the only way he can do this without penalizing the other youngsters in the class is by careful, meticulous planning. Please note, though, that this planning is not overly time-consuming, and that you will be able to work up plans which will be good for many classes, and for many lessons.

THE PLAN FOR THE YEAR

Possibly, a yearly calendar is already available. Many departments have worked on these, and keep them on file. If so, your job is simplified. If not, take your curriculum bulletin or textbook and read it. Either of these will be divided into units. Count the units of work, and the time you have in which to cover them, and you can easily determine the amount of time to allot to each. Consider a year to have forty weeks, and, with eight units of work, you would allocate approximately five weeks to each unit. If some units are shorter than others, vary this by devoting three weeks to them.

You need this type of plan because it is very easy to become involved in a particular topic for too long a period of time, thus short-changing the others. Sufficient class time must be given for every topic you teach. One can "cover" an entire unit too quickly. One teacher we know tried to teach all of South America—geography and history—in one day! It was required in his syllabus that his classes study this material, and he simply had not planned on a yearly basis. This was the only time we have heard of a teacher being this negligent!

DAILY PLANS

As a conscientious teacher, you probably put a great deal of time into making your lesson plans, but don't you find that, as you progress, you need far fewer hours? It is a very rare person who can be a good teacher, however, and not plan fully and completely. The time you spend at this makes your lessons much easier to teach, more interesting to learn, and more suitable to the needs of the slow learner.

In your planning, you must include work for children with varying abilities within the same class. Some children learn more quickly than others, and will be bored if you do not have new material for them. Slow learners often do better at a slower pace. For example, in the teaching of arithmetic you must teach the fundamentals, and then review them again and again for the slow learners. In this way you can be sure they are grasping the ideas you are trying to convey to them. If a child does not understand "ten minus six equals four," he certainly cannot solve a problem involving the operation "six hundred ten minus thirty-six." The brighter child is far more likely to have grasped the fundamental idea after hearing it once or twice than the slow learner. No class consists of children who learn at the same rate; yet it is our job to teach each child. You can most easily do this by setting up groups within your class. This is particularly important in the teaching of reading and arithmetic, but also valuable in social studies or science.

Grouping by learning ability

Let us consider teaching vocabulary to a class which you have divided into three different groups. In the first, you have placed those boys and girls who know the fewest number of words. In the second are those whose vocabularies are better, and in the third are the children who seem to have the best ability to speak, because they apparently know the most words. For each group, you will need a list of new words which you will be teaching to them. However, the method you use may be identical for each group. (You may wish to use the one given in Chapter 5.)

There are certain factors to consider, though, as you establish the groups. Making them flexible and changing them frequently assures that no stigma will be attached to any of them. It is most important that no child feel that he is "stuck in the dumb group." Do not think for one moment that children do not realize which groups they are in. Because of this, it is necessary to change them often, according to the children's particular needs. Be sure that, while you are busy with one group, the others have work to do. We are sure you realize that when children are not occupied, they become rambunctious.

Even if your class is composed entirely of slow learners, you may still wish to utilize the grouping techniques, because in this way you teach children to get along with one another, to live and to work together. This aspect of behavior itself is extremely valuable.

Your plans should be flexible

Your plans should be such that you must not hesitate to add to, or delete from them, if necessary. You will find you will get ideas from the children, which may be added to the lesson. Probably you will use these plans again, and the additions you have made usually add to their value. We have found that using a loose-leaf notebook, with a separate sheet for each lesson, is good. By dating each in pencil, plans can be reused. Leave room for your comments, and additions.

Your calendar will outline the units of work you will cover, and the specific lessons into which these have been broken down. This would then be followed by your daily lesson plans.

SPECIFIC COMPONENTS OF THE DAILY LESSON PLAN

The type of daily plan which follows is one of many. We have found it serves our purposes well, and does not require an inordinate amount of time. It consists of these basic parts:

Aim
Motivation
Concepts
Pivotal Questions
Individualization
Homework Assignment
Warm-up (The warm-up is particularly good in the junior high school and is discussed at the end of this section.)

Aim

It has often been said, "A journey of a thousand miles begins with but a single step." This is true of learning, too. Consider the aims of your lessons, strung together, as the *steps* of learning in the *journey* of the course you are teaching.

The aim should be stated as a question, and preferably as a "How" or a "Why" question.

How can we predict weather?

Why did the colonies decide to break away from England?

How is addition like multiplication? *How* is it different?

What rules help us to spell words like lie, receive, receipt, recipe?

Why did Brutus kill Caesar?

The aim is the focus of the lesson. It must never be above the heads of slow learners. It is the focal point for you, and for the children as well. Make use of it—in your thinking and in your work. Write it on the board or, better still, have the class secretary, or a youngster with good handwriting, place it in full view of everyone. It serves as a beacon. What am I trying to accomplish here and now? What steps are we taking today?

Have the class copy the aim into their notebooks. With the rest of the material you will give them, there is a logical sequence— and learning is far easier in such a sequence. Particularly with slow learners, we must stress this sequential aspect of learning to attain clear, logical thinking—of which these children are capable, if we train them to do so.

When you summarize the lesson, use the aim as the guide. Are your students able to answer the question it posed? As you question them, make sure you call much more often upon your slow learner. Do this in a warm, friendly manner, rather than in a cold, probing way. If he gives you a partial answer, help him to complete it. Always make him feel his contribution is important. In a word, encourage the child as much as possible. You may be able to tap unsuspected sources of intellectual activity. Just because a child doesn't read well does not mean he cannot learn and enjoy your lessons.

Motivation

Motivation is the key which unlocks the child's mind, and each lesson must have it. It is the spark which kindles his interest. Or you may think of it as the bait you throw out. This is the place where your creativity starts. Let your imagination run wild!

Psychologists tell us that there are two basic kinds of motivation: intrinsic and extrinsic. Theoretically, intrinsic motivation comes from within the child. For example, most of us would like to know how to predict weather, and you can utilize this, perhaps, by saying, "Wouldn't you like to know if it's going to rain, so that you won't travel out to Shea Stadium and find the ball game is called off because of bad weather?" You build on those ideas the child is interested in and shows his curiosity about. This is intrinsic—he needs to learn this lesson for himself. But, how often is this true? One percent of the time—two percent, if we're lucky!

Extrinsic motivation is from outside of the child's sphere. You are bringing it to him—presenting him with a challenge, a thought, a deed. You are, hopefully, making him sit up and take notice. The methods are myriad; the results can be miraculous.

Shoot a small rocket (the kind powered by a carbon dioxide capsule), and they'll remember jet propulsion. Bring in a pot and a hot-plate, and make fudge. They'll never forget the "melting pot" concept. Hold spelling bees, and such words as "liquid" and "communication" become important. Give the children as many real, palpable experiences as you can upon which you build their understanding of concepts. This will particularly help the slow child, to whom the comprehension of a concept becomes less difficult if he sees, hears, smells, touches or tastes it.

Motivation is the key to being not only a good teacher, but a great one. Perhaps all of us can't be great, but we can try. And you personally can have more fun this way because your children will enjoy your class, and show their enthusiasm. They will also, if encouraged, contribute by bringing in things of interest, stories, etc. This brings us to storytelling. The children are interested in your experiences—to a point. They would like to hear about the time you were stranded in the house by ten feet of snow, because that is, in itself, exciting. But all too often, stories about oneself and one's family can be dreadfully boring.

If any child, and particularly the reluctant learner, is not challenged, if the work is above his head or out of his realm of interest, he becomes bored, and he feels that he is an outsider—or in today's parlance, "alienated." Then, to nourish his self-esteem, or to get attention, he may become boisterous, rebellious, or antisocial. His raucous laughter, calling out, or fighting will loudly proclaim that he was not included in the intellectual activity of the class. You must be extremely careful to include him in your plans, first by motivating him.

In your plans, your motivations might be:

SHOW A FILM STRIP: "How to Write a Newspaper Article."

OR: Play a phonograph record, "Scarlet Ribbons."

OR: Tell an anecdote: In Salt Lake City, Utah, there is a monument to a sea gull. This city was settled by the Mormons, seeking religious freedom, more than one hundred years ago. The people arrived there, after tremendous hardships, such as bringing their belongings on pushcarts moved, by hand, across the country. Their settlement flourished, until one year, not too long after they had established themselves there, a plague of locusts descended upon them. They saw their crops being consumed—and were powerless to do anything. Suddenly a huge flock of sea gulls came and destroyed the locusts. Remember, though, that Salt Lake City is a thousand miles from the sea!

OR: Photographs from *Life* or *Look* magazine.

OR: Experiment with magnets to show the magnetic field.

The amount of time and effort you put into thinking up unusual things will make or break your lessons. Let your imagination go. Be creative, be imaginative, be innovative! It is here that your knowledge of your subject will help. Bring in the little known facts, the things that make learning fun.

Concepts to be covered

This is the place, in your plans, to fill in all the material you will want to cover. It makes your teaching much easier if you know exactly which salient points you must include. Use an outline form, which is easily read, and which, if you so desire, you can check off.

Include concepts and examples; work in sequential order. This, too, helps you in thinking your lessons through. If your ideas are very clear in your own mind, it is far more likely that you will be able to impart your knowledge to the children.

The following lesson is often useful:

TO SMOKE OR NOT TO SMOKE?

Aim: To smoke or not to smoke?

Motivation: Use one or more of these: Filmstrip on smoking; Advertisements from magazines and newspapers; Actual packages of cigarettes to show the warning on them; Have children read this aloud; Film or speaker from the American Cancer Society.

Concepts to be covered:

A. The reasons people smoke:
To be "one of the crowd"; for something to do—to relieve boredom; to relieve tension.

B. The reasons smoking may be dangerous:
It may cause heart disease, lung cancer or emphysema; It is habit forming; It could be a fire hazard.

C. Statistics in regard to the possible dangers of smoking:
One pack a day; more than one pack a day might be more dangerous; young people start slowly as a rule, but increase so that by the time they are adults they may be smoking two or more packs a day.

D. The part the advertising industry plays:
Tremendous sums of money spent for radio, television, newspaper, magazine and billboard advertising.

E. The part our government plays:
Warnings on packages; limitations on advertising.

When you plan your lessons, refer to other resources, such as encyclopedias, library books, and curriculum manuals. Take notes. so that your work is available to you in the future. Be sure you use more than one source, more than the textbook the children are using. Include material you think the children will find interesting, but be sure it is on their level.

Don't neglect to challenge the slow learners. Give them concepts which are new, and with which they are unfamiliar. Nothing is as dull as constant rehashing of old stuff.

If the boys and girls give you leads, follow them up. They often can show you what they are interested in—"clue you in." Let them! If they ask you a question suggesting a topic, and you possibly can, pursue it! If not, at least answer the question fully. You need not be enslaved by your plan. You may, at some time, have the gratifying experience of having planned a lesson, and, by the time you confront your class, finding to your delight, that in some part of your mind you have new ideas that enrich it, resulting in a far more interesting lesson than the one you had expected to give.

Select the essential points of the lesson. List them in your plan. Then during the lesson, have the students give them to you. Have the class secretary write them on the board, and have the class copy them into their notebooks. In this way you are sure the students have notes on the lesson. Specify, when you wish them to take notes, "Write this in your notebooks." Then watch to see that they are doing this, because in so doing you are actually teaching the children the skill of note-taking and of summarizing. They develop good work and study habits, which are conducive to wholesome discipline.

Remember, most boys and girls simply cannot, by themselves, select the most important points of your talk, nor can they write fast enough to get everything down. Therefore, you lighten your work and, at the same time, structure the lesson for your classes by having the summary put on the board. The slow learner must have these notes from which to review.

Pivotal questions

The key to good teaching is to draw as much material as you can from the children. You do this by constant and skillful questioning. The pivotal questions are your insurance that you will cover the most important points. They may, if you wish, serve as a summary, or as a homework assignment.

Usually pivotal questions are "How" or "Why," "Explain" or "Describe." Rarely are they "What" or "When."

For example, in the lesson just quoted, "Why does smoking make you feel like one of the crowd?" is a possible pivotal question. The following are, as well:

"Why do scientists believe smoking may cause lung cancer?" "Why do so many people ignore the warnings the Department of Health, Education and Welfare issues in regard
to smoking?"

Using five or six pivotal questions, you will find that you can review the entire lesson. Your pivotal questions must be varied so
that there are some so simple even the slow learner can answer
them easily.

Individualization

To individualize your lessons, you must know what the children's talents and needs are, and wherein their deficiencies lie.
Most frequently there is a reading problem. Therefore, to teach
such a child, use discussion and even lecture, rather than expect-
ing him to learn new material by reading it.

To help with his problem area, you may wish to give him individual attention during the assembly period, during the play period, and during class time (Illustration 2-1), while the rest of

Illustration 2-1

the class is engaged in doing written work—for example while they are writing the summary. Indicate, in your plans, "While class summarizes, work with John." If there are a number of pupils with similar needs, group them, and then teach that particular group. Assign research on the damage cigarettes might do (in the lesson just given); while some of the children are doing this, you might work with another group on their reading. Indicate this, too, in your plans thusly: "Work with Group B on reading skills."

When you have bright children in your class, it is well to awaken their social sense by having them assist the slower children. Close association with bright children often helps the slow learner. A fine young writer of our acquaintance said she had received her best grades when a teacher wisely seated her with two students who habitually received good grades. The teacher fostered the development of a friendship between them. They walked home together, did their homework together, and the weaker student, stimulated by the companionship of the brighter girls, found that learning could be a pleasant experience and, indeed, even a source of enjoyment.

If you have slow students who have other talents, give them assignments utilizing them. For example, a child who draws well might do posters on the possible dangers of smoking. Others might make models of normal hearts or lungs, and of those that might be damaged by cancer. This fulfills their needs to accomplish, to achieve, and builds their self-esteem. They will come to school less reluctantly if their work is on display. The perceptive teacher will try to find ways to help the slow child to find his gifts, and will include these, too, in her lesson plans.

Homework assignments

There are a variety of homework assignments which you may give, keeping in mind the problems of your slow learners; remember, though, that to learn to read, a child must read; to learn to write, he must write. Modify the assignment to fit the child, but be sure he has work to do, and is motivated to do it. You may wish to help him select library books related to smoking, which are within his comprehension. Magazine articles are excellent. If his reading is very poor, you may wish to rewrite the articles to simplify them. However, to avoid giving the slow learner work to do is to cheat him of the opportunity to learn.

Here is a list of assignments from which you may choose those fitting your class, and its needs:

1. Answer specific questions on the lesson covered.
2. Read:

    a. In the textbook, a portion of the text relative to the topic under discussion;
    b. Introductory new material, on topics to be taken;
    c. Review material already covered in class;
    d. In-depth research on any of the categories above.

3. Reports or projects covering a larger quantity of work.
4. Drawings, paintings, montages or other art work relative to the topic under discussion.
5. Creative writing relative to the topics being studied.
6. Experimentation—in relation to social studies (Consumer education, for example) as well as in science.
7. Scrapbooks, other collections of related material.
8. Study assignments—preferably written. For example, when an important examination is to be given, review for it by asking the pupils to outline their notes, and then study them. Simply studying can be forgotten more quickly than some sort of writing.
9. Making up puzzles, such as crossword, or number arrangements, dioramas, pictures, models. (Here, too, creativity is wonderfully effective.) Even the poorest students will often bring in beautiful scrapbooks, for example, in social studies. Encouraging the use of imagination makes teaching a joy. Your children may delight you by bringing in surprisingly good examples of creative work. I remember one incident when the topic was "Indian Villages" (part of the language arts curriculum). The teacher must have stirred the children's imagination, for the next day a child brought in a beautiful Indian village made of cardboard, clay and paper mache. The probability is that the child had the as-

sistance of the other members of the family in constructing the village. This, too, is desirable, for an intellectual note had been struck at home (successfully), sparked by the teacher. When the child appeared with the village, he was as proud as a peacock—so was the teacher as she placed it on the windowsill—and it was a source of pleasure to everyone who entered the room.

10. Slogans and posters. For example, in the lesson on smoking, a child brought in a magnificent poster, with the following slogan:

Are You Public Enemy Number One?
Are You Wanted for Murder, Mr. Cigarette?

There are certain cardinal rules in regard to homework:

1. It must be gone over in class, and evaluated.
2. It must be of value—not simply "busy work."
3. It should not be so simple that it insults the children's intelligence. This is particularly true of the slow learner.
4. It need not be assigned only one day in advance. Reports, charts, projects, panel discussions, or plays all take time. Indicate this to the pupils—that these will be graded, and the grades counted for more than single homework assignments. It is possible to give an assignment due two weeks hence—with an equivalent amount of credit.
5. It is advisable to have the assignment stimulate interest in the subject. However, some review and drill is always valuable—providing it is not assigned too often.

Warm-up

In junior high school, a warm-up exercise (placed on the board before the class enters the room) is an essential. It serves to settle the class and to get them started working. (This will avoid disciplinary problems.) Very often, if there is no work for them to do, they will wander around the room and get into trouble. When children have work to do and, are trained to do it from the very beginning, they will usually enter the classroom, sit down and get to work. Again, the work must be such that the slow learner is capable of handling it, for his own intellectual benefit, and for maintaining wholesome discipline in the classroom. The warm-up should not be the same every day. Any of the following are good devices:

1. Vocabulary building. List new words on the board, with their definitions. Have children use them in sentences. Or, use words which you want to review with the class. In this case have the pupils give you the definitions. Vocabulary building connot be over-emphasized; one measure of intelligence is a person's vocabulary.
2. Review of material previously covered; have the children answer questions.
3. Matching questions; multiple choice; true or false.
4. Writing a summary of the previous day's work.
5. Drawing or interpreting a diagram or simple graph illustrating some point covered in the lesson.
6. Reviewing important basic concepts—measurements, dates, multiplication tables.
7. You may want to duplicate a short paragraph and have the pupils select a title; or pick out the topic sentence; or write a summary.
8. Drawing maps.

To use the warm-up most effectively, tell the class you will quiz them on the facts you have covered, and then do so about once every two weeks. In this way you maintain wholesome discipline, and you cover the subject matter. This leaves you more time during the lesson for working on concepts, and to work individually with the slow children. You also help to develop good work habits. Idleness is defeated, together with its accompanying evils.

Remember, though, the warm-up must be part of the class routine. It must always be there! It must be reviewed. Give the class five minutes to do it—not more. While they are busy, you may take the attendance, and do any other chores you must attend to. However, you must also watch the class, because if you don't, there may be a few children who will not bother to work.

After the five minutes, immediately review the answers the children have given to the various questions, and then proceed with the aim of the lesson. You will find, more often, an attentive, interested group—if your questions have been challenging.

SUMMARY

You may enjoy comparing your plans with other teachers, and discovering which methods and techniques they have found to be valuable. We can all benefit from other people's thinking and experience. There are strategies for teaching slow learners which have worked for other teachers, and might be just what you need. Don't be reluctant to ask or to suggest an interchange of ideas— to "talk shop" with your friends and colleagues (Illustration 2-2).

Illustration 2-2

You may also find that groups of teachers can combine related topics from different subjects to present to the same class. For example, in the junior high school, we find that language arts and social studies teachers, working and planning together, can be most effective. For the slow learner this provides the link between subjects which he needs. There is no reason why a composition in history or biography, current events or government cannot be graded for content and for written English. At the same time, a class studying American history might be reading *Giants in the Earth* in their language arts class. Combining forces, and planning together, some teachers have found their subjects becoming far more interesting to themselves and to their children.

By planning your lessons so that they are within the range of the slow learner's interest and comprehension, you make it possible for him to learn. The aim of your lesson, usually in the form of a question, is the guiding light. The motivational devices are the impetus which will entice his attention—and consequently they should be varied, original and, above all, stimulating. To teach concepts, remember that any actual experiences you can give your slow learner will accomplish far more than mere verbalization, for it is by actually doing that we learn best. You help him to crystallize his thinking when you ask pivotal questions, when you drill deftly and interestingly, and when you summarize succinctly. By placing notes on the board, and having him copy them, you are furnishing definite material for him to review—so that he may help himself, or enlist the aid of members of his family.

Give homework, which you have carefully planned, and be sure that it is checked daily, graded occasionally, and praised whenever possible. Let us give the slow learner feelings of belonging, feelings of accomplishment and achievement by planning work to suit his special needs and talents, and let us do all in our power to make school a desirable place for him to come to—lest he become a dropout, the symbol of our failure as educators.

3

discipline and the slow learner: controlling your pupils until they develop self-control

A prerequisite to teaching slow learners successfully is achieving control of the class. This word "control" does not necessarily mean a silent room, with children bent intently over their work. Nor does it involve a teacher lecturing to a group of boys and girls who are watching him as if mesmerized. Nor is it meant to imply a hushed, still atmosphere, so often experienced in an overheated room.

What, then, does control mean? It indicates the establishment of a climate for work within the classroom. Work suited to the varied intellectual levels of all of the children; work that is planned to include and meet the needs of every child. Youngsters should be participating actively in the lesson; yet they do not call out answers or make other comments. They are involved, thinking and working; if necessary they may speak to one another, but they do so quietly, so that they do not disturb their neighbors. In a heterogeneous group, it is the slow learner who is most often uninvolved—who becomes the disciplinary problem—because he is resentful, bored and feeling neglected.

The concept that the teacher represents the figure of authority in the classroom is most important. He may not be at the front of the room, or even conducting the lesson, but his presence or influence must be felt by every child until that child attains self-discipline. This is the aim every teacher should strive for—to help his children become self-directing, self-controlled. The most effective discipline is thus imposed by the children themselves, because they are actively involved and interested in the work which is going on, and are not resentful, bored or neglected. In this chapter we shall endeavor to assist you in bringing self-control to your children by using a positive approach, by never accepting poor behavior, by handling your own discipline, by being eminently fair, and by making your teaching as interesting to all of the children as you possibly can.

APPROACH THE CHILDREN WITH A POSITIVE ATTITUDE

They are interesting human beings, whom you are instrumental in molding. They are not youthful monsters, trying to make your life miserable—although even the best classes may behave in this manner if they are not properly trained. Show them that you expect them to behave and work in an orderly way, that you respect them as individuals. It is a joy to enter a classroom, find the children already working, and say to them, "Hi! How are you today?" and have them reply, "O.K.," or "I have a cold," or "Not so good after that lunch." Do you answer them? Of course, "What are you doing for the cold?" No long discussion, but a show of mutual concern. Once I told my class, "I'm upset today, so please be cooperative. My daughter has been sick for a week, and I'm very worried." The commiseration, the interest, even the remedies suggested by the parents (because, of course, the matter was talked over at home) were very gratifying.

NEVER ACCEPT POOR BEHAVIOR

When you tolerate disruptive actions, you give the entire class license to misbehave. What one child is permitted to do, you must allow the rest to do as well. Therefore if there is any infraction of rules, you must immediately deal with the child who breaks them. Children sense your reaction to them. They know when you are afraid of them, and also when you like and accept them, and they respond to these emotions. Even the most obnoxious child is responsive to kind words, to discussion, to individual attention—if not immediately, eventually.

After you have your class introduce itself to you, you may wish to say, as I did, "I'm glad to meet you. I know we are going to have a pleasant year working together." Haven't you found, in your teaching, that the "we" concept is vital? One successful teacher we know tells her homeroom class, "I have two families. I have my children at home, and I have you in school. We, too, are a family. If you have any problems, I'll try to help you. Talk to me about them. I may not be able to solve them, but I promise you I will try. But I expect loyalty and cooperation from you in return." Did she get it? Not 100 percent of the time, but far, far more often than not. Children need to feel they belong—and this was one of this teacher's methods for giving them this feeling.

HANDLE YOUR OWN DISCIPLINE

Each school has some system of referral for handling problems. However, the more of them you are able to handle yourself, the more effective a teacher you are, and the stronger you become. It may be necessary to send for help, but do this *only as a last resort*. It is a confession to the children of your own ineffectuality in handling the situation.

Let us return to the actual classroom. The term begins and the classes you teach are well-behaved, or reasonably so. But eventually, "that day" comes when they don't settle down to work after they enter the room. You remind them. Still Mary Smith and Johnny Jones are noisy. You must speak to both of them. "What seems to be the trouble?" So often teachers will speak to John, and not to Mary or vice versa. That's wrong, because it's unfair.

This brings up a most important concept in dealing with children. They will respect you, and react favorably to fair play more than to any other kind of treatment. "Teacher's pets" have been despised since time immemorial. If you can avoid showing partiality, you will earn a reputation which will be of tremendous value to you. I have seen more children, of all ages, cry out, "But it isn't fair." Exert every effort to be as fair as possible—it means so much to the children.

Sometimes this requires much soul searching. People, normally, respond to other human beings, as individuals, and usually in different ways. As teachers, however, we must treat all of our children the same way, or as nearly so as possible. For example, when you appoint monitors, make sure each job rotates, so that no child has it longer than another. When you praise one child, remember that others need praise too. Our slow learners must be given tasks they are capable of performing and their efforts must be respected and commended. Help, do not hinder by discouragement. If you find children seeking favor, gently but firmly, discourage it. You will more easily earn the love and respect of all of the children by being strictly fair.

Back to John and Mary. Is a gentle rebuff enough? If not, what next? They persist. Ask them to see you at three o'clock. Send a note to their homeroom teacher reminding the pupils you expect them. When they come in, explain to them that they were taking away time from the rest of the class, time which cannot be spared. Discuss the importance of education, of their work, or of their future careers. Use this opportunity to become closer to them. (Don't, though, become too familiar.) They are not contemporaries, though they love to feel as if they are. Try to determine, however, why they are problems and what is driving them to behave so badly.

Next day, lo and behold, Mary is still talking out in class. You feel hurt because of the time you spent working with her. What you don't realize is that Mary may never before have been treated by a teacher with love and understanding. Try again. You will find you need a well of patience and compassion, but you, yourself, will grow and mature in these situations. And the method works! Not always, but most of the time—unless you are dealing with children whose problems are so severe they cannot be reached at all.

If after these talks it seems you need some parental assistance, tell the child, "I may have to speak to your mother or father." Warn him before you actually communicate with the parents. The threat may be enough. Apropos of threats—always do what you say, or don't say it. Pupils see through idle threats. If a pupil asks you not to speak to his parent, by all means give him another chance, but put it in those terms. His behavior must improve immediately, or the telephone call will be made.

If you must speak to a parent, telephoning is better than writing. In your conversation, be sure to show your interest in the child. If you are vindictive, you will accomplish little. You must truly try to obtain the parent's cooperation. The conversation might go:

"Mrs. Smith? I'm Mister Greene. I teach your son James, English at Johnson Junior High School."

Wait for a sign of recognition. If it isn't forthcoming, then say, "I hope I'm speaking to the correct Mrs. Smith." Next say something good about James: "He has always looked nice." "He is an intelligent boy." "He usually tries to cooperate." In this way you get the parent "on your side."

Then come to the point. Perhaps you would put it, "We're having a bit of a problem in class. James has been talking aloud to his neighbors, instead of raising his hand. He misses doing his work, and takes away from the time allotted for teaching. Do you think you might discuss this with him?"

What are you accomplishing with this? You have worked with the child, and you have made the parent aware of a problem. Of course, if your whole class is unruly, this procedure is very time-consuming. This is the reason we suggest you start as soon as necessary.

As mentioned before, you may have to punish more than one child—even the entire class. Try to avoid this unless it is absolutely necessary. But if you can't, or if there are several culprits, scold all of them. You must be fair!

If the telephone conversation is not successful, the next step you might try is writing a registered letter to the parents, asking them to come in for an interview. As old-fashioned as this sounds, it still proves to be effective. Your letter to the parent should state:

> I would like to see you in regard to your son James' school work. I have set aside time at 10 A.M. Friday morning, October 13. I hope this time is convenient. If you cannot keep this appointment, please notify me and I will be glad to make another at a more convenient time.

Set up your appointment two or three days in advance, and then mail the letter! Do not send it home with the child—because the chances of it arriving are a bit slim.

During the interview with the parent, show your interest in the child. Ask such questions as, "How does your child behave at home? Have you had trouble with him before?" Add such comments as, "We both realize that in today's world, his education is particularly important. How can *we* help him? This is what he does in class: He . . . , he . . . ." Let the parent know you have spoken to the child, tried to help him; but it hasn't been too successful, that now you need the parents' help. It is a most unusual parent who will refuse, even today.

Make note of all of the steps you have taken. We call this an anecdotal record. It can be very concise.

DATE	OFFENSE	ACTION TAKEN
9/12	Talked out in class.	I spoke to James in class.
9/14	Repeatedly talked out—five times in one period.	I spoke to James after school.
9/26	James talked to his neighbor 20 minutes, instead of doing his work.	I telephoned parent.

The purpose of keeping such a record is simply to show the steps you, the teacher, have taken in helping that particular child. There are some severely maladjusted children who cannot function in a school situation. The anecdotal record is needed to make any referrals to outside agencies, as well as to the school guidance and administrative personnel.

It is possible that, even after doing all of these things, you still are having difficulty with some child, or children. Now you might say, "In all of the years I have been teaching, I have rarely had to refer pupils to the principal. Must I send you? I really don't want to—unless it is absolutely necessary." In many schools there is an administrator who is in charge of discipline. Before you make the referral, review what you have already done with the child, and request help, simultaneously, from the disciplinarian and from the guidance counselor, because this type of behavior is often indicative of a need for special guidance.

The procedures outlined are often effective. The most important point to bear in mind, at all times, is that you are the figure of authority, and it is sometimes necessary for you to teach a respect for authority to children who have never been taught it before. It is a challenging task, but a most rewarding one. To earn the respect and love of young people is one of the greatest joys of our profession.

KEEPING YOUR CHILDREN BUSY AND INTERESTED

Haven't you seen children misbehaving because they have not been assigned work to do? You can't expect them to sit quietly if they are unoccupied. Why should they? They are healthy, young and full of life and energy. For this reason, as soon as they enter the classroom, there should be work for them on the board. It provides you with an opportunity to take the attendance, prepare your needs for the lesson, check homework, or do any of the other tasks you deem necessary.

While working with your slow learners during the lesson, provide an assignment for the rest of the group. If you don't do this, some children will inevitably find something to interest them which might have a detrimental effect upon the discipline of the others. In one art class we observed pint-sized cans of paint sailing through the air. The teacher was helping one child; both were oblivious to the ball game going on around them.

We said before that a good teacher always maintains order. If he can hold the interest of the children, the battle is nine-tenths won. Your best and most effective weapon is to be interesting. The question, then, is how?

Be sure you are teaching on the children's level, reaching all of the children

There is nothing so boring as being in a class where you comprehend little of what is going on. Try listening to a foreign language radio program and see how long it holds your interest if you do not know the language. The teacher must try to speak a tongue which each child understands. He tries to reach every boy and girl. In order to do this, he may ask, "Are you with me? Do you understand?" Encourage them to respond.

In my teaching of science I found that slow children could not learn much from reading. They had to be taught, using other tools and devices. They could also, I noted, do far better on oral quizzes than written ones. Their problems were many, but I found that I could and did teach them. I will never forget the time "Obstakilution" appeared as an answer on a written quiz. The correct spelling would be "Optical Illusion," but the intention was valid. Slow children can be stimulated to think in the same way as you would stimulate average or bright youngsters. It is our job to do this—and it can be an interesting, challenging one.

Make your work apply to their lives, as much as possible

If a class is doing a lesson on graphs, have them plot the growth of their community, or the comparative baseball averages of their favorite teams. Lessons stressing consumer education are practical as well as interesting.

Do not rely solely on your curriculum bulletins for ideas. Courses of study are an absolute necessity—but you must *build* on them. Think up your own gimmicks, tricks, interesting lagniappes to throw in. You will find them throughout this book. Puzzles, games, magazines, books are all valuable, and children love them. (So do adults, don't they?)

The price of chicken feed is very dull compared to the price of going out on a date. The profit made on a pair of shoes is not half as stimulating as the profit made on the sale of a guitar. George Washington looked unhappy because his false teeth were made of wood and hurt him. How do you think you'd feel under the circumstances? As much as you can, relate your teaching to their experiences. A social studies unit on the history of the community in which you live is of far more interest than a discussion of a place no one in the class has ever seen. If the latter is part of the curriculum, though, you can teach it as a unit. "Why would living in Hawaii be different from life here in the continental

United States?" Take your pupils on trips, to give them experiences you can later use in the class.

Children are people, and the more you can involve them in your teaching, the more you can enthrall them. You can often use the question, "What would you do under the circumstances?"

a) In an English lesson, after a story.

b) In math, after solving a problem.

c) Franklin Delano Roosevelt was handed this problem: Did he want the development of a weapon so dangerous it had the explosive power of a million tons of T.N.T.? He said yes, and the atom bomb resulted. What would you have done under the circumstances?

d) We live in a time when there is grave danger of a food shortage which could kill millions of people throughout the world. What should we do, and how should we do it?

The ramifications of such problems are tremendous, and one can teach much more than the specific factual knowledge if one handles the topics well. We can develop in our students feeling and concern for their fellow human beings. What is more important?

Work to build a success pattern

Far too many of us teach an entire class, without trying to get through to each individual pupil. The result is that many of our slow learners are in a vacuum, and may not have the slightest idea of what is going on in the classroom. We lose them, and our work is lost. How can we avoid this?

a) Frequent questioning—pose each question to the entire group. Get as many pupils as possible to try to answer. Don't call on the same pupils constantly; try to call on everyone in the course of several days or a week. Many of your simple questions should be directed to the slow learners. Let your manner be gentle and encouraging, never sarcastic or damaging. By belittling their efforts you might actually cause them to "block," thus closing the doors of their minds to learning.

b) Ask questions they are able to answer. Try to stimulate the slow learners to think—not just the few "hand-wavers" each class has.

c) Try to build up the self-esteem of each child in the group. Encourage them all to bring in things of interest. We call it "Show and Tell" in the lower grades, and actually the same concept is involved in the conversation pieces many of us keep on our coffee tables at home. Children have brought, to my science classes, such prizes as a deer embryo, the skull of a steer, an iguana lizard (live), and countless other things. What is particularly significant is that each of the items listed above was brought in by a "slow learner."

d) Try to build this success pattern by assigning work that each child can accomplish. For example, list some relevant topics on the board. Allow the children to choose things which interest them—they are more likely to participate if you offer them some choice. Even slow children can do oral interviews, take notes and report back to the class.

Each child, however, must be made to feel he can contribute, that he is capable of completing some tasks successfully. We have found work in the industrial arts classes good, in this respect, for often children with academic difficulties can do beautiful work in the shops.

If you are teaching reading, find material which is written simply, but with concepts which are of interest to children of the ages you are teaching. It is indeed an insult for a fourteen year old to have to read "Jim and Sally went to the store." They can learn far more from "The rocket blasted off. It had been on the launching pad for days and days. This was the trip we had been waiting for. This rocket was heading for the moon." If need be, prepare your own material for your slower children. Never, but never, insult a child's intelligence. Allow him to try to fulfill your expectations of him.

Produce plays wherein each pupil can take part

The self-esteem of everyone must be nourished, not just that of the star. In fact, avoid stellar roles, if possible. When you produce a play, try to work with another teacher so that one can be backstage to supervise, while the other is rehearsing the pupils in their roles.

It is possible to write your own plays, too. Every child can contribute a little something, particularly in the area of language arts. Here, there is frequent opportunity to work out a class project.

Look for techniques which hold all the children's interest, never forgetting the slow learner

A school or class magazine requires much work, but can give many rewards in return. Some children draw, others compose puzzles, and still others can write stories, poems, articles or conduct interviews. Mothers, or even members of the class, may type the stencils, and copies can be given to each pupil, and used for reading material.

What happens when a class enters your room overly excited, and you must calm them down? You can do this with the work which you have previously written on the board. If you do not care for this technique, you must find another, but you cannot teach a group of youngsters without first settling them down. Nor can you stand and wait for them to become quiet. It is far better to give them work to do, and get them started doing it.

Each child is a part of the entire class and no one can be a law unto himself

We must get this concept across to the children. The welfare of the entire group is what we should and must aim for. For example, in one case we know of, one boy shouted during an actual fire. Pandemonium ensued, and several children started kicking and pushing. In the panic which resulted, two children were hurt badly enough to require hospitalization, not from burns, but because of the infraction of school laws by one of the unruly children who began the shouting.

Fire drills must be absolutely silent! They are practice sessions for emergencies, which arise at the most unexpected moments. We must train our pupils to handle themselves as if they were soldiers responding to commands. They must see for themselves that they have responsibilities to every other person in the school. At this time, complete silence is an essential to the welfare of the entire group. When children themselves realize this, they become self-controlled. At first, you will find some of the children not responding. Don't lose heart. As you work with them, the rest will "come around." Your influence, your direction, and above all your attitudes are important.

Where does self-direction and self-control enter the picture? When you have taught your pupils to work at the tasks assigned, and when they are truly interested in what is going on in the classroom, there will be a climate in the room which you, they, and everyone entering the room will feel. It is one of work, and of pleasure, and interest in working. If what you say is vital to the class, and one pupil disrupts, another child will "shush" him. If you have given the pupils the feeling that you believe they are responsible human beings, acting in an adult fashion, they will behave accordingly, providing their work truly involves them, catches their interest and holds it. Try this experiment: Find the most interesting puzzle (on the class's level, of course) and give it to the group to do. Then walk out into the hall and listen. Or set up a class newspaper (in any subject area), divide the class into groups, making sure that they know what they are to do, are capable of doing it, and observe from outside the room. Will decorum be 100 percent perfect? Probably not. But try and see how close it can come.

Generally, an unruly group is an uninterested group. Interest them and they become completely different. This was very graphically brought out in the book, and film, "To Sir, With Love." When remedial fourth grade work is done with ninth graders, how can we expect them to feel? They need it, you may well argue. True, but it must then be given on their level. One can make up material simple in language, but significant in concepts.

One personal experience: When teaching science I discussed, with a group of very retarded readers in the seventh grade, the concept of prehistoric life. They were fascinated as the lesson progressed; from this came a trip to the Museum of Natural History. (I would tell the children, "Watch the tyrannosaurus carefully. He nods and says 'Hello, children! Hello, Mrs. Karlin! when we come in.'") Every child learned to read the word "dinosaur" after seeing it in print twice. Other ideas followed; a study of fossils, for example. So did reading about them. The children learned how intellectually stimulating learning can be, and how exciting. The pupils didn't dream of being unruly. When you, the teacher, have something like this going on, you truly savor how great being a teacher can be.

Learn of your children's lives

Teaching is a many-splendored thing. One of its fulfillments is to be an ever-present help to the slow learner, who needs your sympathy and understanding perhaps far more than any of the other children. Get to know him well; invite his confidence. We all like to talk about ourselves—so do the children. Let the intellectually impoverished child tell you about his problems in school, his living conditions at home, his family life. Perhaps he has emotional blocks; possibly you might ferret out their causes, and consequently succeed in removing them. Remember—we teach with our hearts as well as our minds.

> In one case a drunken father perpetrated cruelties at home which made it well nigh impossible for the child to concentrate upon his school work. Because the teacher had taken a special interest in the little boy, inviting his confidence, talking at length with the child, arranging an interview with the mother, and then contacting the proper social agencies, the situation was remedied, and the child, who had innate intelligence, changed from a slow to a normal learner. Knowledge is power—and it was the teacher's understanding of the little boy's serious problems that helped to solve them.

SUMMARY

In this chapter we have discussed the various methods of attaining wholesome discipline, showing that it is never punitive. There is every possibility that your slow learners may easily become disruptive influences in your classroom. In order to prevent this, you must approach these children with a positive attitude, one that will awaken a mutual respect between teacher and children. If you insist that every child adheres to fine standards of behavior, you will always maintain a firm hold on your class; and you will be giving your children training in self-discipline. You must try to handle all of your discipline cases yourself, for the children will quickly sense your inability to do so if you repeatedly call for help. Above all, you must keep your children busy and interested; this applies particularly to the slow learners. Never forget to keep within the range of both their interest and their comprehension. Effective teaching of the slow child is generally far more successful if we furnish personal experiences rather than lectures. Plan your lessons around their lives, assigning work to them which they may successfully complete. This will give them a sense of accomplishment and satisfaction. Remember that, far too often, the slow learner is the forgotten child in the classroom. By including him in a play which you may wish to produce, you help him to gain a sense of self-esteem and belonging.

Search tirelessly for strategies and techniques which will hold the interest of every child in your class, regardless of his I.Q., remembering always that by enticing and maintaining the children's interest, you will avoid discipline problems.

By implanting habits of self-discipline in the children's minds, you teach them to act effectively in the event of emergencies, thereby insuring their personal safety as well as the safety of the group to which they belong. This is particularly true during fire drills.

Learning about your children, their problems and their needs, may enable you to help them shed their labels as slow learners, and to improve the entire course of their lives.

4

teaching the slow learner
to communicate
through
the language arts

There are none so blind as those who will not see, and there
are no children so impoverished as those who are unable to
communicate. While the communication skills should be taught
in every area of education, they are formally presented in the
subject referred to as "language arts." Formerly called English,
the name was changed because it was recognized that there
were four distinct skills or arts involved—listening, speaking,
reading and writing. It is assumed by many teachers that the
child learns the first two in his early years, from his family. However, educators have realized, only recently, that there are a
great many children who are deficient in these fundamental tools,
and slow learners are almost invariably among them. Methods and
techniques for teaching all of these skills follow with the ad-
monition that you must not ignore any of them, for the child
who lacks these abilities is truly handicapped. It is difficult for
us to imagine ourselves unable to communicate, but we can approach an approximation of this if we imagine ourselves in a
foreign city, with no knowledge of the language. Even then, it
would be far easier for us to make ourselves understood than it
is for a child who has a meagre knowledge of words and a poor
command of the English language. We cannot be blind, ourselves, to the needs of our slow learners in this most important
area—language arts.

TEACHING TO LISTEN

A. *Talk with your slow learners.* This basic method of teaching is very often ignored. Children need to hear and use good speech, and what better way is there than by conversation? When you are teaching slow learners, use vocabulary they will understand easily in the beginning; then introduce words they are not familiar with, and so build a familiarity. Discuss with the children various events and topics, in keeping with their ages, interests and intelligences. The shy child, the reticent one, is often desperately in need of being spoken to, of being drawn out and taught to actually listen and speak.

B. *In many homes parents read aloud to their children for hours and hours.* But in other homes there are boys and girls who are never or rarely read to. We suggest you read aloud to your children, and have youngsters who are capable, do the same. Select stories, articles, or poems which will capture and hold the attention of the slow learner. Use all of the dramatic talent you possess—remembering, a good teacher is also an actor or actress. You must make the children listen, because while listening they are learning.

C. *Encourage the children to ask to be read to by their brothers and sisters.* You may permit them to read to one another, working in pairs, or small groups. For materials use books, newspapers, or magazines. When a child feels he is able to do so, allow him to read to the entire class.

D. *Play records or tapes of readings or of dramatic presentations.* Be sure they are within the range of the children's comprehension and, therefore, will not prove dull or boring to them.

E. *Show films which contain good speech, and which will be appealing to the children.*

F. *Recommend television programs which will be meaningful to the children, and which contain clear speech.*

G. *Listen to famous speeches.* Recordings are available of world famous speeches, read by professional actors. (Doesn't Raymond Massey, portraying Abe Lincoln, come immediately to mind?) By utilizing these recordings children hear immortal words, well spoken. You may wish to introduce readings from Shakespeare, or from the Bible, remembering, of course, to suit the quotations to the intellectual abilities of the children. Hearing such English helps to "tune" the children's ear, and at the same time develop an intellectual pride in the boy or girl. He can tell his family, "Today we heard a scene from Julius Caesar. Did you ever hear of him?" One mother told me this—adding, "My son was shocked when he found we had."

TEACHING CHILDREN TO SPEAK

It is absolutely essential that every teacher assist any child who needs help in learning to speak clearly and effectively. The impressions we make on people are tremendously influenced by one's appearance and by his speech. The brightest person gives an entirely erroneous picture of himself if he is unable to communicate. This area of education must be taught until each child masters it. The era of the teacher doing all of the talking must be over, and the process of learning must be like a two-way radio —broadcasting back and forth, and broadcasting in the clear, lucid tones of the radio announcers—or as close to that as we can approach.

Our primary goals must be two-fold—fluency and clarity of expression. Some children have already reached these, but often you will find your slow learner has not. To encourage all children to speak, even the reluctant ones, we recommend you try the techniques which follow.

A. Practice conversation. This is discussed under "Listening."

B. "Show and Tell," or a variation, is excellent on almost any level—certainly in the elementary school, and surprisingly in the upper grades, where it would be referred to as "How to earn extra credit by bringing in, and talking about, objects of interest." Ask the children to bring in things they would like to talk about. Is there a stamp collector in the class? He might bring in some of his most interesting specimens. Souvenirs, postcards, books, dolls, almost any objects are worthwhile, if a child wishes to discuss them. Books, magazines, even newspaper articles may be discussed.

C. "Let's Tell a Story." The story we propose is told by all of the children, getting even the slowest learner to contribute. Begin with a dramatic, thought-provoking sentence. Have each child think of possible additions. Then call on one to give his. Continue until an entire story is told. Encourage the children to be humorous, mysterious, truthful or outrageously fictitious. In fact the latter is an excellent way to experiment with this method. For example, we might say, "Having lived in the time of the dinosaurs, I had a boy friend named Tyranno. He was a loveable fellow, but I couldn't marry him because he was too short. I was a mere slip of a dinosaur myself, about twenty feet tall."

If you find that your children are unimaginative, add material yourself. Try to make this as pleasant an activity as you can, and encourage the children to enjoy it.

D. Develop public speaking. Few people are comfortable when called upon to speak in public, and yet this often proves necessary. Assist your children to develop poise and self-confidence by having them speak in class. However, assign topics about which they will feel the least amount of anxiety. Find subjects in which children are interested. For example, "My Favorite"—ball player, ball team, television program, sport, country, food (and how to prepare it), singing group, game (and how to play it), pastime, book, movie, movie actor (and why), or public figure. Hero worship shouldn't be dead.

Perhaps the children will enjoy preparing a speech, pretending they are tour guides taking visitors on a trip around the city. Suggest they include such comments as "George Washington didn't sleep here. He stayed awake all night—the traffic made so much noise!"

Help your slow learner in the preparation of his speech, and make him as confident as you can.

When you discover a child who has specific speech problems, individual attention is to be desired. If you do not feel qualified to teach, in the area of remedial speech, seek the assistance of specially trained personnel.

E. Rehearse tongue twisters. These word games do serve a purpose. They make speech easier; while our young ladies often have very facile tongues, the young gentlemen do not.

"Peter Piper picked a peck of pickled peppers," "She sells sea shells," "How, now, brown cow, grazing in the green, green grass," are all time honored, but still have value.

For fun, you may wish to inject this into your work: "Mardon me, padam, may I show you to a seat in the chack of the burch. Isn't it a cheautiful burch? Many thinkle peep so. Oh, mardom me padam, this pie is occupewed."

Or, ask your children, "What is a myth?" After getting a series of responses, tell them, "No, a myth is a female moth."

F. Develop plurals. Give your children the singular, and have them call out the plurals. Then "catch them." Such a session provides hilarity and facility in speech:

> Plural of mouse is mice, then the plural of house is _____.
>
> Plural of goose is geese, then plural of moose is _____.
>
> If the plural of box is boxes, then the plural of ox is _____.
>
> If the plural of fox is foxes, then the plural of sox is
>
> _____.

G. It is not necessary to try to eliminate all regional accents, but it is essential that each child speak clearly enough to be easily understood. We feel you must work with any child whose speech is not readily discernible, helping him to achieve clarity. If a child has a foreign accent, which makes his speech difficult to comprehend, you may wish to work individually with him, helping him to eliminate it. It is imperative to remember that no child should ever suffer from embarrassment or feel inferior because you are working with him on his speech. Aim for clarity, and for understandability. How tedious it becomes to listen to a friend or relative whose speech is not discernible! Though his subject matter may be fascinating, if he is not easily understood, listening to him becomes difficult, and unenjoyable. Slurred speech will act as a detriment throughout the child's life. You can effect the most far-reaching education by helping him in this area.

WRITING

In teaching children to compose, we must keep one point foremost in mind—they will achieve far more if the writing is purposeful. "We will write compositions today, and three will be chosen for the school magazine (or newspaper). The others will become part of your portfolio," you announce to your class. You may have the children write letters, or themes, poems or invitations, but all with a reason. They may prefer to keep scrapbooks of their work, rather than portfolios, or you may use the creations to decorate your bulletin boards (Illustration 4-1). But above all, give each and every assignment a purpose.

Illustration 4-1

The following method for teaching composition is one we have found successful with individuals of all ages. We ask that you try it once, before you judge—because your reaction upon reading it may be negative. You may feel that you are putting ideas into the children's minds. This is true, but you will find that these help the slow learner a great deal—and that he progresses from those ideas to his own.

A. *Seat the slow learner near the teacher's desk.* Make him feel that he may consult her as often as he wishes, with reference to the selection of his topic, use of proper words or correct sentence structure, or any part of the work in which he needs help. A warm, gracious manner toward the child will awaken his confidence in his teacher, and will tend to preclude any timidity on his part to approach her and ask for assistance.

B. *Seat the "class writer" at the rear of the room.* (Choose him as early in the term as possible. He is the child with the talented pen, the gift of words, and the power of verbal expression.) Leave a vacant seat beside him, to be occupied by any child who wishes to obtain help from him while working on his theme. This arrangement will encourage cooperation and class rapport.

C. *Motivate the composition.* In the selection of a subject for your composition, be sure that your motive is of vital interest to both the children and the teacher. For example, each year the social service organization B'nai Brith holds a contest offering prizes for the best composition on "Brotherhood." You may use this for motivation, as the purpose of the composition assignment. Present this information to your class, adding, "It would be nice if one of us can win this contest. We all know how important the subject is."

D. *Get the children's thoughts to flow.* Before any child does any writing, discuss the subject. You may begin the discussion by asking, "What are some thoughts or quotations about brotherhood? What is it?" Or, you might ask the children to think of the words to "America the Beautiful," and then ask, "What is meant by the last two lines of each stanza?"

> And crown thy good with brotherhood
> From sea to shining sea.

Perhaps you might care to contribute the words of Seneca, spoken hundreds of years ago: "We are members of one great body, planted by nature in mutual love, and fitted for a social life. We must consider that we were born for the good of the whole." Or Sir Walter Scott's, "The race of mankind would perish did they cease to aid each other."

Write these quotations on the board. If you would like others, have a child consult a reference book on the subject. Then ask the class what thoughts these quotations bring to their minds. Write the best ones on the board, not in the form of a composition, but spreading the ideas all over the board at the front of the room, explaining as you do why one word or expression is better than another.

"Which is better?" you ask. "Brotherhood is important to us." Or "Brotherhood is the cement which binds our nation together, uniting people of different races, creeds and colors."

When, as a result of the general discussion, the blackboard is covered with views, ideas, words and worthwhile expressions contributed by the children and supplemented by the teacher, ask for a volunteer to tell the class the gist of his composition. Some child, probably the class writer, will be eager to do this. Then, because thought begets thought, another child will be motivated to do the same, and then another. When the air and the blackboard are filled with stimulating thoughts, the class may begin to write their themes. While the children are working, you might invite the slow learners to your desk; discuss their compositions with them, and work with them individually, giving them as much of your time and attention as is necessary, since their need for your help is greater than that of the other children.

As soon as they have been completed, hang up some of the themes at the front of the room. It may be possible to display the work of the slow learner, and if it is, by all means do so to encourage him. It may not measure up to the quality of the others, but we must build up the confidence of the slow child. Every composition should be entered in the competition run by B'nai Brith. Have the children write copies to keep in their portfolios. Do not deny any child the right to enter the contest; you may find you have winners in your class, which offers a great deal of satisfaction to the children. You may also decide to use some of the themes in the class newspaper. (Do not use the winning themes. Give other children—and parents—recognition.)

E. *Utilizing other topics, the same procedure may be followed:*

1. Choose a topic of interest to the children.
2. Motivate it by stating the purpose of the writing.
3. Recall the sayings of great men that are appropriate to the topic. (You may have to search for one, but it is worthwhile.) Or you may make a provocative statement yourself. You might also use quotations from newspapers, magazines, or books.
4. Write these quotations on the board.
5. Encourage the children to contribute their ideas.

6. Write these ideas all over the board, spreading them around.
7. Point out to the children why some expressions are more descriptive than others.
8. Ask for volunteers to give their classmates the gist of their compositions.
9. Have the children write their themes.
10. While the class is so engaged, work with the slow learners.
11. Exhibit the best compositions.
12. After the work is completed, check with the children by asking, "Have we fulfilled our purpose in writing this composition?"

Unexpectedly this method brings forth a diversity of ideas and expressions, first verbally and then on paper. While some of the children may repeat ideas, they will add their own variations, and we have obtained surprisingly good results from the slow learners, for they need not flounder. (How often does even an adult have difficulty because he lacks a starting point!) By giving the child direction, you help him and you will find he gains momentum—ideas are stimulated, thoughts are stirred and the result is fruitful.

You may utilize this technique with any grade. Of course you would suit the subject matter to your particular class and the quotations, too, to the intellectual level of the children.

F. *Use vocabulary to motivate compositions.* One successful teacher used her vocabulary lessons to introduce to the children words which were related in meaning. Then, when the words had been mastered, she suggested themes they might write utilizing them. She found that they were able to do this, and actually make the new vocabulary part of their working knowledge. For example, she taught her slow learners words describing emotions —nouns such as fear, hate, love, anger, anxiety, happiness; verbs such as depress, elate, react and respond.

Then when the time came to write the compositions the motivation of the assignment was "Introspection—determining how I feel about things." The children suggested other titles, such as "My emotions," "Controlling my emotions," "How people's emotions work for or against them," and "Should people try to hide their emotions?" The compositions definitely reflected the vocabulary work, and the children were able to see that words are the tools which we use to express our thoughts (Illustration 4-2).

Illustration 4-2

Similar lessons with other words would help the slow learner in the same way. There are a plethora of vocabulary building books available in inexpensive editions, which will give you ideas for this kind of lesson planning. Be sure you keep the children's level of comprehension in mind. Present material with which they will be able to cope, and words they will be able to use in their everyday lives.

G. *Letter writing is easily made purposeful.* For example,

1. Writing friendly letters:

a. To friends, who really exist. These may be Pen Pals, or friends of friends, students in other schools or even celebrities.

b. Writing to service men—who so much enjoy getting mail.

c. To people who are ill—homebound, or hospitalized. There are many elderly people who enjoy corresponding with youngsters.

d. To the editor of the local newspaper—stating the writer's views on subjects of current interest.

2. Writing business letters:

a. Requesting information about other nations from the embassies, delegations and consulates.

b. Requesting free literature from large corporations such as the Ford Motor Company, Kimberly-Clark, General Motors.

c. Applying for jobs. (Explain that this is purposeful, because it is something almost every person has to do at one time or another, and that the more practice one has, the better one is at it.)

3. Filling out application forms—for jobs, for the same reason as item #3 above.

4. Answering letters from others—business or social. (Another very practical aspect of letter writing which children need to know.)

5. Writing invitations to parents to visit the school for various functions.

H. *Assign topics for compositions.* Often teachers are at a loss for topics. We should like to suggest these:

1. Why I think we should . . . . (Anything from the sublime to the ridiculous—from "Why I think we should return to walking on all fours," to "Why I think the United States should go off the gold standard").
2. If I inherited a million dollars I would (may be humorous or truthful).
3. The most unforgettable person I know is . . . . (Incidentally this may be assigned as a fictional account, or a nonfictional one.)
4. If I could go to any place on earth, I'd like to visit . . . because . . . .
5. I love, hate, envy, admire . . . because . . . .
6. How do I feel about our President (Governor, Mayor)? (Particularly good during times of controversy.)
7. Exhibit a photograph, a piece of sculpture, or a painting. Have the children tell the story which the object brings to their minds.
8. Exhibit several psychedelic prints, zodiac signs, or pictures

of mythological beasts, and have the children write stories about them.

9. Select several antiques and exhibit them. Have the children write their reactions to such objects as a china doll, a sword or a tintype.

10. How can I, as a young person, work toward peace in the world?

11. How can I work to help my own community, and the people living in it?

12. Give the children an initial sentence and have them continue it. *For example:*

   a. As I boarded the train, I knew something unusual was about to happen to me, for I could feel it in my bones.

   b. The day was sunny, with a cool breeze blowing, and one could feel adventure in the air.

13. "What do certain words mean to me?" Mention words such as freedom, democracy, love, brotherhood.

14. Play a piece of current music and have the children write their thoughts about it.

15. "What responsibilities do I have toward myself?" "Toward my family?"

16. "Why do I think school is valuable?" or "Why do I think school is a waste of time?"

17. "How is my generation different from my parents'?"

18. What America means to me.

19. The character I read about who is most real to me is . . . because . . . .

20. Why I feel close to my brother or sister, or why I don't feel close to my brother or sister.

21. Select a newspaper headline, and have the children write an imaginary story about it.

22. Play phonograph records such as "Sound of Silence," and have the children interpret the lyrics. Use recordings by the Beatles, for example.

23. Take an imaginary trip; when children have read of a place, have them write about their "visits" to it. For example, if they have read of the "moors" in *Wuthering Heights*, they might "visit" that area of England.

24. Have the children write safety plays, to be performed for the children in the lower grades.

I. *Introduce the class to research.* When assigning research to your children—and the fourth grade is not too early—be sure you teach the boys and girls specifically what you expect them to do. Take them to the library and instruct them in the technique they must use. Too often teachers neglect to do this, and the children do not know how to proceed. Having taught the manner in which the assignment is to be done, make sure all of the children understand it.

Doing research projects serves many purposes. You are teaching skills which the children will find valuable. You are making writing purposeful and, if the topic is interesting, you can motivate them to do a thorough piece of work. The choice of subject, though, is very critical. Can you relate it to the pupils' lives? Subjects such as riots or violence are to be avoided, but many areas of current events are excellent—medical developments are very exciting at this time.

The topic need not be related directly to the curriculum. The raison d'être for this report is to teach research techniques, so that even a remote connection is adequate. Drug addiction, for example, interests young people. Why not work directly on prejudice and discrimination (the negative aspect), or the brotherhood of man (the positive)? Remember, your goal is to get quality work on interesting subjects.

Having done all of these things, you will find it helpful to:

1. Give three or four weeks for the assignment, but check it at least twice to be sure each child is working on it.

2. Hold conferences with the children, keeping a record of their progress. (Just a note—outline done, reference books used, etc.)

3. To further motivate the pupils, tell them that the authors of the best papers may, if they wish, present their papers to the class. (If you assign this, it becomes unpleasant, but put this way, it becomes a reward.)

4. Demand, and make sure the class understands that you are seeking, quality work.

5. Mark the papers carefully, but generously, giving consideration to the capabilities of the author. It gives a great deal of encouragement to the slow learner who needs it so desperately.

6. Allow any pupil who wishes to do so to present his paper.

If he would like to, permit him to invite his parents to hear it. You will find this may bring out some of the children's hidden talents.

7. Remember that you are stressing quality. Far too often teachers will not bother to give this type of assignment to reluctant learners. These children are rarely pressured to do good work, and consequently do not ever make a great effort. Perhaps you might like to introduce the topic in this way: "I realize this assignment is not really on a junior high school level. It really is more like a college assignment." (Watch the students perk up at this. It is true. And yet they can do it and will—if you insist upon it and if you teach and help them. If they are in fourth grade, tell them it's sixth grade work, etc.) If they wish to type their reports, and have the facilities available, by all means permit it.

8. After the papers have been reported on, exhibit them in the classroom, in the school library, or in any other prominent place in the school. This accomplishes much toward building the pupils' self-esteem and self-worth. It shows other pupils what their schoolmates have accomplished.

9. Allow the slow learners to use pictures from magazines, but be sure written work is included.

In giving such an assignment, remember there will be a great variation from child to child and from class to class. However, once you teach your students what you expect, you will find you can get good work. Never accept sloppy, careless work from any child, because by doing so you are guilty of intellectual discrimination.

TEACHING POETRY

If "music is the food of love," as Shakespeare tells us, then surely poetry, too, nourishes the heart. The reading of poems is particularly desirable with the slow learner who is often emotionally impoverished. The rhyme and rhythm of the verse form stimulate both thought and emotion, while the pause that generally occurs at the end of each line gives the child a moment to think, and facilitates reading. If the poem is wisely chosen, he will enjoy hearing and subsequently reading it. The younger children like such narrative poems as "The Owl and the Pussycat," while the older boys and girls thrill to "The Highwayman." Choose poems which will appeal to your children—for their rhythm or rhyme, for their beauty, and for the moral message they may carry.

Because poetry is a channel for the emotions, you will find, if handled wisely, that it has an ameliorating effect upon discipline. Poetry, like music, hath charms to soothe.

We have found that teaching poetry effectively is not difficult. We suggest you try the following procedure:

1. Make copies of every poem which your children are to study (if they do not have them in their textbooks) and have them keep these sheets in their notebooks.
2. Prepare this lesson by studying the poem, familiarizing yourself with the lines, so that when you present it to the children, you are able to do almost a dramatic reading of it. Give the reading as much dramatic fervor as you can muster.
3. As you read it aloud, have the children follow you on the printed page.
4. Ask for volunteers, and permit the children to read aloud the parts they liked best.
5. Follow this with a discussion of the poem: have the children select the most important ideas and phrases. Emphasize the message, pointing out the images the poet gives us, and his use of words to convey moods and emotions.

It is possible to follow up this type of lesson with a dramatization based on the poem. We did this, on one occasion, very successfully with Joaquin Miller's magnificent poem, "Columbus." The method outlined above was followed, and as the interest and enthusiasm for the poem dawned in the children's faces, we asked them whether they would like to give an assembly program based on this poem for Columbus Day. They were very eager to do so. The actual performance consisted of a child reading each stanza of the poem, followed by a group of children acting out the message contained therein, suiting the words in prose, to the story of the poem. When we reached the part beginning, "My men grow mutinous day by day," it was not difficult to dramatize, for there were discipline cases in the class whose interpretations of the lines were well nigh perfect. The final verses of the poem served as the finale, spoken in unison, dramatically, by the entire class.

Try to bring to your children the drama, the verve, the imagination to be found in the world of poetry, for you will find they will enjoy it tremendously. Let us never lose sight of the fact that poetry is written fundamentally for enjoyment, for stimulation and for moral elevation. Let's not convert lessons in poetry into difficult intellectual exercises but let the children feel the rhythm of the poem, its emotional appeal, its dramatic quality, its power and beauty.

Illustrating poems

Many poems contain beautiful imagery. Call attention to the images of the poem you are reading. For example, "The road was a ribbon of moonlight over the purple moor." Doesn't this bring a magnificent scene to mind? If your children care to, they may illustrate such images. Do not ask every child to do this, but rather suggest that anyone who would like to paint or draw this scene may do so. We must be careful that we do not cause children, for any reason whatsoever, to dislike poems, for then we defeat our own purposes.

Background material

Very often children, and adults too, are affected as much by the story behind the poem as by the actual work itself. We cite Edgar Allan Poe, and the terribly sad story of the death of his lovely young wife, "Annabelle Lee." A wonderfully effective teacher gave this unforgettable lesson to our daughter, who repeated it to us, and had the entire family almost in tears. It is guaranteed that that child, and her family as well, will never forget the poem and the tragedy. Not only did this gentleman teach the children a series of magnificent verses, but he also developed their feelings of compassion and love, which are far more important.

Writing verse

You may have children in your class who are able to express their own feelings by writing verse. If this is true, encourage them, assist them and praise them. However, never tell your boys and girls, "You must write a poem for Abraham Lincoln's birthday." This is sure death for the muse.

A poem entitled "Brotherhood" was written by an eighth grade student, and subsequently published in the school literary magazine. It could never have been written "to order."

Writing a class poem

Another kind of lesson which fosters a love of poetry is writing a class poem. Announce to your children that you would like to experiment with this, and have them suggest subjects. Decide with them what, specifically, they are going to write about. Next have them suggest ideas and write these on the board. Then ask for sentences and record them. Discuss the relative merits of these contributions. If need be, contribute lines, words, or phrases yourself. Ideas will be generated rapidly, for children love forming rhymes and creating images. Your children and you will probably put together a pleasing poem; if you do, duplicate it, distribute copies; and illustrated by one of the children, display the poem on the class bulletin board.

Making "poetry pouches"

This is another activity children enjoy. At the beginning of the term, give the boys and girls large manila envelopes, and encourage them to decorate them attractively, including the words "Poetry Pouch" on each. During the course of the year, whenever your children find poems, or parts of poems which they enjoy, whether they hear them in class, or read them elsewhere, they are

Brotherhood

You speak of me in your highest
    places of learning,
And write of me often,
And then you butcher me.
You lie
But not to me
To yourselves...
You tell yourselves how advanced
    you are
And how civilized,
But open your eyes and look at the
    world you live in.
You say you believe in me
But slowly I die and lies are no
    medicine.

Once in a long while I am born
    again
In the heart of a friendly old man,
In the easy smile of a child.
And maybe,
With hope
I can look onward
To a time
Where I am not nurtured
In a politician's speech
Or a school assignment,
Where I come easily and naturally,
Where I belong.

* Reprinted from *Prall on Parade*, Anning S. Prall Junior High School, Staten Island, N. Y.

to copy them or cut them out, and place them in their pouches. Any original verse is also kept there. We followed this method, and every so often had a poetry hour, which was devoted to the reading and discussion of these poems. The teacher read some of her favorites to the children too, keeping within the range of their comprehension and interest. The original verses written by the children were accepted for publication in the school magazine, and an anthology of verse was compiled, using the pouches as the most important source of the collection; these were exhibited, and whenever visitors entered the classroom, the anthology and the "Poetry Pouches" attracted considerable attention.

Teaching vocabulary through poetry

Teach the poem as suggested above. Then ask the children to find the words that are new to them, in the poem. List these on the board, and working with the children, determine the meanings. Have the children find the lines which contain the words, and try to develop the meanings from the context of the poem. You may have them use dictionaries as well, if you feel this is necessary. The children should then write the words and their meanings in their notebooks. They should copy the poem, or use the duplicate sheet to underline each new word.

A study of words such as this will enrich not only the children's vocabularies, but also their hearts and minds, for a familiarity with the poem, a "nodding acquaintance" is built.

Games with poems

Your slow learners will enjoy little games played with poems with which they are familiar. Write the poem on the board, omitting the last word of alternate lines. It may be a poem such as " 'Twas the Night Before Christmas," which most of them know, or you may do this with poems which they have in their notebooks or textbooks. The children then copy the poem, filling in the last word. For example:

> O Captain! My Captain! Our fearful trip is done
> The ship has weather'd every rock, the prize we
> sought is _____.

This is a simple way of reinforcing the learning of the vocabulary and the message of the poem.

Poetry as a moral force

Let us not overlook the tremendous power of poetry as a moral force in our classroom. Some of the most beautiful lessons taught in the history of mankind were written in verse form, teaching the lesson of universal love; it is a lesson which must be learned and relearned in the classroom today if we, as human beings, are to survive.

Let us search our memories and our books, find some of these magnificent lessons and place them before the children so that the power of these thoughts will reach their hearts and minds. You may have the children look for poems containing such sentiments, or you may wish to give them the quotations and have them print them attractively. Display them throughout the classrooms, and even in the halls and offices of the school. Such poems as "Abou ben Adam" by Leigh Hunt, or "A Man's a Man for All That" by Robert Burns, or "A Creed," by Edwin Markham, are excellent examples and you will find many, many more. By having them exhibited in places where the children will see and consequently read them, you keep this important message constantly before their eyes.

For many years, we had exhibited in the front of our classroom in Edwin Markham Junior High School these lines, written by the man for whom our school was so proudly named. It is the first stanza of his poem, "A Creed."

> There is a destiny that makes us brothers
> None goes his way alone:
> All that we send into the lives of others
> Comes back into our own.

(Reprinted by permission of Virgil Markham)

How could our children fail to be impressed?

SUMMARY

We have divided the language arts into the communication skills—listening, speaking, reading and writing. Reading is discussed at length in Chapter 5. It is absolutely essential that each area be taught, for no child can afford to be lacking in any of these; yet unfortunately it is the slow learner who often is.

We can teach children to listen by talking with them, by reading aloud, by playing records, showing films, watching televised programs, and by playing recordings or doing readings of famous speeches.

To instruct them in proper speech, we can use games such as "Show and Tell," or "Let's Tell a Story," by having the children make speeches, and by using tongue twisters and drills.

To foster writing skills, we have included a method for teaching composition, containing a special technique to stimulate the thoughts of the slow learners. Another method involves the introduction of vocabulary words as the basis for theme writing. Letter writing, specific topics for compositions, and a strategy for building vocabulary are discussed.

We have found, too often, that poetry is ignored, and yet we feel it should have a definite place in the education of the slow learner. We have included a method for teaching it—and suggestions for illustrating poems, for teaching background material, for the composition of a class poem, and for teaching vocabulary through poetry. There is also a game, or simple exercise, which may be used very effectively with slow learners and which they will enjoy. We discuss poetry as a moral force—surely one of the most vocal—in our fight for "life, liberty and the pursuit of happiness."

Each of these techniques may lead you to think of adaptations, or you may use them exactly as they are outlined. But most of all, we hope we have conveyed to you the need to teach each of the four basic areas, making sure that every one of your slow learners will leave your class improved in the ability to receive and to transmit ideas to others through the spoken and the written word.

5

teaching
reading in every
subject area

Even today, there are sixteen year olds in our schools who have never learned to read. Reading specialists are needed to teach such pupils, of course. But there are a great many boys and girls who read poorly, and who need assistance in improving their reading skills. We believe this, then, is the task of every teacher.

When a pupil's reading is retarded, what suffers most is his self-image. He feels he is a failure, that he has already "flunked out" of school, and of life. Very many retarded readers behave in just this way. Their self-pride is so severely damaged that they do not seem to be able to pass any subject, although they are of normal intelligence.

The child who has difficulty reading is alienated from the time the problem manifests itself. This may be as early as the second, or even the first grade. Because of the emphasis our educational system places on reading, it is assumed that if a child cannot read, he cannot learn. We hope that you have discovered for yourself that this is not true—that, utilizing unusual methods, you can initiate his active participation in other aspects of the learning process. But what can we do to help remove the stigma? Many things! You have probably developed some devices of your own to teach reading—and used them successfully. The following techniques are given in great detail, so that you will be able to adapt them easily to fit the needs of your children.

On the elementary level, every teacher should stress reading as one of the most important parts of the daily curriculum. The skills which follow may be covered at that time. In the higher grades, however, despite its great importance, reading is often relegated to the language arts classes, where it receives only a portion of the time—large or small, depending on the decision of the teacher or the syllabus. Because the effects of the inability to read are so far-reaching, because the slow learner usually falls farther and farther behind in this area, we suggest, and strongly urge the teaching of reading in every subject area.

Inasmuch as reading is the key to all knowledge, its mastery is the first, vital and fundamental step in educating the slow learner. How else, besides through a printed page, can the thoughts of a person dead for two hundred years come to us— fresh and clear? Almost every person alive in our society must know how to read—the mechanic to consult an instruction manual, the physician to keep up with the latest developments in medicine, the salesman to know the products his company handles, and the housewife to follow recipes or to give penicillin to a sick child.

> "You know your chances to succeed in life are slim," the guidance counselor told the handsome blonde boy. *He didn't answer.*
>
> "The jobs you can get are limited to unskilled work, for the most part." *Still no response.*
>
> "When you drop out of school, some people call it dropping out of life. Do you need the money so desperately?"
>
> "No."
>
> "Does your family?"
>
> "No."
>
> "Are you in trouble with the police?"
>
> "No."
>
> "Then why, in heaven's name are you leaving? You're just sixteen. There are many boys around here your age who are trying to graduate. Why aren't you?"
>
> *He looked around, making sure the door was closed. He moistened his lips, tried to speak, but couldn't. He tried again.*
>
> "It's just——"
>
> "Yes?"
>
> "It's just——well, I can't read."

This is an extreme case, a relatively unusual one; but it is not fictional.

The methods which follow have proved to be extremely valuable. We will discuss a method which will help your children to enlarge their reading vocabularies by approximately five hundred words per year. Children may be trained to recognize the definition of a new word when it is included in the selection they are reading. This method is outlined under the heading "Using conceptual clues to learn the meanings of new words." Reading comprehension is another area which we find we can teach most successfully by breaking down into specific parts. You will find methods for selecting the main idea of a paragraph, for reading and thinking critically, and for summarizing what has been read. For practical purposes there is a selection on reading and following printed directions, and using the contents of a book. If, as we fervently hope, our children continue their educations, this skill is an invaluable one. We conclude the chapter with a reading program which demands the pupils read, and we suggest a method which will motivate them to seek books, and to learn to improve their reading by developing a love for reading.

We will start, as we believe you should, with a program to improve the child's image of himself.

BUILDING A SUCCESS PATTERN

Motivating the reading skills program

Before using any of the skills outlined in the following section, we urge you to discuss with your children the reasons for working on their reading—in today's jargon, "tell it like it is." It would be wise to tell your children, "In order to achieve success in school, and in almost every type of work which follows it, you must know how to read. Very, very few of the people who are not able to read can earn enough money to live comfortably." Discuss this, drawing out the children's experiences, continuing until you have made the point.

Then proceed with the next concept: "If we, as a nation, had a military enemy, how might we win a war against it?" Elicit responses from the class. They will possibly answer, "We would use bombs, or tanks, or guns." Your response can be, "In other

words, by using weapons." Then, place the word "weapons" on
the board. Ask for other ideas. You may bring forth the reply,
"Strategy." Write that on the board, too. Continue with the questioning until the children express the idea of "divide and conquer." Make note of that phrase too. Then relate all of these to
reading. "Let's consider not being able to read as our enemy,"
you say. "We have weapons to fight it," and you hold up exercise sheets. "We have strategy—which I will give you. Can anyone see how we would divide and conquer?" Try to bring forth
the idea that reading may be broken down into many skills, and
that each, individually, may be learned and conquered.

Every child, and particularly our slow learners, would like to
"slay the dragon," the standardized reading test. Ask the class if
they would like to learn how to use a "spear of knowledge." Then
proceed to teach them by utilizing the first skill in the following
section, regarding vocabulary. Since you use the format of the
test for drill purposes, you actually are preparing them—and they
will recognize this very quickly, and respond favorably to it.

After working on this skill, announce to the children. "We have
a plan for teaching you to read better, comprehend more, and
learn many reading skills. It contains many exercises similar to
the ones we have just done. It is in the nature of an experiment.
Who would like to participate?" It is an unusual child who can
reject the idea of being part of an experiment, and you may use
this as a selling point, and then use the more important approach
that these methods do work; they will succeed, as they did with
the vocabulary. All children want to succeed desperately. But
because as slow learners they have met failure so often, they may
lack enthusiasm—until you show them that they can learn, can
comprehend, can read (Illustration 5-1).

Recording the results

Begin by giving pretests—using questions requiring the skill you
are going to teach. Have the children grade their papers. (You
may wish to use the system outlined in Chapter 11.) Assure the
class that you never consider these pretest grades—that they are
for their personal use only—and have the children record them

Illustration 5-1

on their rating sheets. Then, teach the skill, do drill work on it, and give a test at the end of the unit. Again have the grades recorded.

You may wish to use the following form, which you can duplicate, and distribute:

SKILL SHEET			
Reading Skill	Date	Test or Pretest	Result

Make sure the quizzes are simple enough to insure good grades. A long list of entries of marks of 90 to 100 percent is excellent. If you are dealing with children whose reading has been retarded, they need this success to overcome the damage their self-images have suffered.

As part of the success pattern, when your youngsters have done reports, as will be suggested, read them, and grade them only if they are of high quality. If they are poor, return them to the children, with suggestions for improvement. Have the changes made, and the material returned to you for grading. The boys and girls are able, in this way, to raise their marks, again earning the success they need. And, incidentally, they will love you for being so kind, and so generous, and for doing what every fine teacher should do—teach and encourage.

TEACHING READING

With the exception of the section on reviewing unfamiliar words, the methods which follow will be useful with children of all ages. The experience chart can tell a sophisticated story as well as a simple one. The articles you select for the individualized reading program should be determined by the age and interest level of the children for whom you are preparing it. By using more than one method, you can make your instruction in reading a more stimulating experience.

Experience charts

Prepare a large chart by drawing horizontal lines on it, about 8 inches apart. Use a pencil for this.

With the children decide on a topic which interests them. Relate it to their lives. It may be a trip the class took, or a television program they saw, something which they heard about in the news reports, or a school happening.

Have the children compose sentences. When a sentence suggested is simple, but clearly expresses the ideas you and the children are trying to bring out, print it on the experience chart, using a crayon or a felt pen. Introduce new reading vocabulary at the rate of approximately five words per chart. If you find this method enjoyable, you may do a new chart every other day. It is one way in which you can relate the children's experiences to their reading material.

Have every child read the chart; then have them copy the story into their notebooks. You may then instruct them to turn the page; on the other side write the new words again, one under the other. Next to each, have the child compose a short sentence.

By using this method, you are able to foster writing and spelling as well as reading.

Prepare your own reading materials

On the children's level, prepare copies of materials which will interest them. Have a variety of different subjects; in this way it is relatively simple to individualize the work for your slow learner. Distribute these sheets, and have the children read them silently. Then have them draw or paint illustrations for each. Next have the children read the sheet aloud, giving each child an opportunity to perform. Instruct the children to save these reading materials for review purposes.

For sources, you may write your own stories, or you may utilize books, newspapers or magazines. These are easily chosen to appeal to the children, and should be of current interest.

Review unfamiliar words taught during the week

Print each word in varying colors on a sheet of oaktag, about one foot square. Using a set of these words, give each child an opportunity to read one word. Call on each child, and if he is able to read the word correctly, he is given the card, and a star. Continue this procedure until no cards are left. The child who has the most cards wins a small prize—a box of crayons, a pen, etc. The children who incorrectly read a word are expected to remember the word they missed, because after the prize has been given out, you put the cards around the room on the chalk tray, and have them select the word they missed. When they are able to do this, they too get stars.

We have found that stars, stamped into the children's notebooks, or on their papers, are an excellent device for use with children in the lower grades. They are easily stamped, and are visible rewards which the child may show to his parents; for the teacher they are a simple, quick means of showing approval.

The children, the parents and the teacher all derive pleasure from them.

In the upper grades, very good results were obtained with a stamp saying, "I'm proud of you. This is a fine piece of work." Another which proved useful had the words, "This shows improvement. Keep trying!" These comments are particularly valuable to the slow learner, whom we must encourage every step of the way.

Individualized reading

To meet the reading needs of every child in your class is not an easy task. However, if you are willing to spend the time, you can set up a sequential library, which enables each child to proceed at his own reading pace.

A. Select reading materials the children will enjoy—at various levels of difficulty. Let us say you will need approximately 150 articles, ranging from simple to complex (in terms of vocabulary and comprehension). Choose your materials from magazines, newspapers or books, or write them yourself. But this material must be of interest, extreme interest, to the children, if the program is to succeed.

B. Place each article in its own booklet, and write on the inside front cover a listing of the new vocabulary. On the inside back cover, place an assignment. Vary these assignments using:

1. A series of questions to be answered.
2. A group of terms to be matched.
3. A list of questions to be completed.
4. A diagram to be interpreted.
5. A graph to be drawn.

After a child has read any article, he must write a short summary of it using the new vocabulary listed at the beginning of the booklet.

C. On the front of each booklet, place a number. Draw this in large numerals, with a felt pen.

D. For lesson planning, use a chart. List each child's name and put a row of boxes next to each name. In these boxes you will write the number of the booklet the child is to use. After he has read the story, he is to hand in the assignment. You then grade it, and circle the number to show that the work has been completed, and the child given credit. A new number is then placed on the chart next to the child's name: i.e.,

Jones, Mary   (6,) (9,) 14
Smith, Bill   (34,) 40

Some assignments will, of course, be more difficult to read, and will require more time than others. However, let the children work at their own pace.

E. Choosing the material is critical for the success of this method. Old textbooks are an excellent source. *Life, Look, Sports Illustrated,* and such publications cannot be overlooked. Keep in mind, too, that boys and girls are interested in different things, and you must include and assign material geared to both sexes.

For the slow learners with reading difficulties, you will need articles which will hold their interest, yet are simple and straightforward. O. Henry's stories are effective—but be sure they do not contain dialogue of a difficult nature. (Mark Twain, for example, is not easily read.) Fiction and non-fiction may both be used. Do not be afraid to go into other subject areas. Science and science fiction may prove to be very popular. (You will find children asking, "Can I read #34? Billy said it was great.") Tales of the Old West or mysteries are good. Sherlock Holmes' or Edgar Allan Poe's stories are stimulating. From the magazine section of your local newspaper to the old issues of *Sports Illustrated,* from the current *TV Guide* or the classics, you will find materials to use.

As we said, we are aware of the time it will take you to prepare these pamphlets, but they may be used for months, and, after they have outlived their usefulness with one class, may be used just as effectively with another. You may ask your children to be on the "look-out" for usable articles, and give them credit when they bring them in.

The individualization you are able to achieve for your slow learners is very fine, for it is possible to choose simple articles with specific children in mind, and then have them proceed to more difficult material. There is absolutely no stigmatizing, nor finger-pointing, for you may assign simple materials to the other children as well.

Make the booklets uniform in size, and store them in shoe boxes. Assign a child to act as librarian, and to keep the booklets in order. Then, when you begin your reading lesson, the children consult the chart, select their work and begin. You are free to assist the slow learner, so that he may learn new skills, and may "catch up" to his more successful classmates. Go over his written work with him, to be sure he has successfully completed it, and shows that he comprehends it.

Class libraries

If you can, set up a library within your classroom. You may be able to do this with books borrowed from the school library, from your own collection, from the children, or from the contributions of the Parent-Teacher organization. Encourage your children to borrow books as often as possible.

TEACHING VOCABULARY IN LANGUAGE ARTS

One realizes how very important word knowledge is when one remembers this is one of the major criteria used to measure intelligence. Bring out the fact that, very often, intelligence tests are, for the largest part, vocabulary tests. We can help our pupils, in almost every instance, to increase their scores, and more important, to increase their ability to communicate.

Word wallets

To make a "word wallet," have the children decorate manila envelopes, and label them, with their names, class, and "My Word Wallet" prominently displayed. Then supply each child with index cards. When he learns a new word, have him write it on the front of the card and also compose a sentence using the word; then place the definition on the reverse side of the card. These cards are kept in the wallet, read at "vocabulary time." This device works particularly well in the second and third grades. It may, however, be tried with older children too.

Meet a new family of words each week

Tell your children they will be meeting a new family of words each week. Utilizing prefixes, suffixes and root words, you can teach a large number of words which the children can retain because of the relationships. For example:

1. *Psyche* (mind) as in psychology, psychiatry, psychedelic, and psychosomatic.
2. *Ology* (study of) as in biology, geology, ecology, embryology.
3. *Trans* (across) as in transport, transatlantic, transcribe, transcript.
4. *Tele* (far away) as in telegraph, television, telescope. (There is a little joke which is applicable, "What are the three fastest means of communication? Telephone, telegraph and tell-a-woman!")

Suit your choice of prefix, suffix or root to fit the comprehension of the children. You may vary this to fit the needs of the slow learner. On the junior high level, he might master "biology" and "geology," but embryology might be too difficult for him.

Should you wish to, you may have contests to see which children can think of the largest number of words with a common prefix, root word or suffix; for example, write "graph" on the board—the children would then suggest: photograph, phonograph, telegraph.

Point out to the children that occasionally they will meet marriages between families. "Telegraph," for example, unites "tele" with "graph" (for "to write far away!") both of which we have met in their separate families. We create new words, too, from prefixes, suffixes and roots. "Telecast," for example, from "tele" and "cast."

Teaching children to love words

"Everything else disintegrates; words last forever."

Many words have fascinating stories attached to them, and the investigation of these will add interest to their study. Dr. Wilfred Funk has done much work in this field, and his books are to be recommended to you, the teacher, and to your children as well. To capture the boys' and girls' interest, tell them such tales as the origin of the word "sandwich."

> The Earl of Sandwich loved gambling so much he was always reluctant to leave the gaming tables—even to eat. He ordered roast beef placed between two pieces of bread, which he could eat while he played, and thus brought immortality to his name; and, at the tables in Las Vegas, people still eat roast beef sandwiches for the same reason.

Teach one new word a day

Choose words which have practical value to the children. You may have the children look up the definitions, or you may give them the definitions and have the youngsters write sentences. Break the words up into their parts—the prefixes, roots or suffixes. Try to develop an exceptionally interesting sentence for each word to help the children to remember it. Have your slow learners suggest sentences, whenever possible, and have these printed on large sheets of oaktag, and exhibited.

BUILDING VOCABULARY IN OTHER SUBJECT AREAS

Within every unit of work which you cover, have one vocabulary lesson. Select approximately ten new words from the text, or from other printed material which you are using; you may vary the number, but more than ten words per week is excessive.

A. List the words on the board, and ask the pupils to define them, in their notebooks. Give them time to do this. If they don't know every word, have them leave blank spaces, which they will fill in later.

B. Then have the definitions written on the board. Some pupils will be able to supply more definitions than others. If all of the students know more than six of the words, this vocabulary list is too simple. If they know less than four, it is too difficult.

C. Be sure you use each word in the lesson, at one time or other. Perhaps you will have the students read the word, or use it in your discussion. When you give a homework assignment, include every new word. The next day again use the words in the "warm-up." Learning of new vocabulary must be reinforced. To do this, make these words part of your lessons whenever you can.

D. Use this form for giving vocabulary quizzes once or twice a month:

SELECT THE CORRECT ANSWER FROM THOSE LISTED, AND CIRCLE THE LETTER IN FRONT OF IT.

1. A *sofa* is . . .

    a) path   *b)* sponge   *c)* couch
    d) roll   *e)* protest

2. *Former* means . . .

    a) shaped   *b)* in the past   *c)* artistic
    d) stiff   *e)* large

3. A *verdict* is . . .

    a) decision   *b)* jury   *c)* trial
    d) question   *e)* slogan

4. *Nonchalant* means . . .

    a) free   *b)* graceful   *c)* casual
    d) laughing   *e)* worried

E. Because we are interested in encouraging our pupils, in building a success pattern, if the results of the quiz are not high, give it again. This is not a waste of time, because you reinforce the learning at the same time that you help to improve the self-image.

F. You will find that you can make words interesting if you present them dramatically. How better to illustrate the word *surprise* than by telling a mystery story which includes it. We personally observed youngsters learn "trephining" and "mesomorph" as a result of a trip to the Museum of Natural History. The verve with which you teach words will imprint them on your pupils' minds. Whenever possible, choose colorful words which will lend themselves to this. Remember "Words are the soul's ambassadors. While other things perish, words live forever."

G. As an added motivation, once or twice a month you may wish to conduct a competition, similar to an old-fashioned (but still fun, and useful) spelling bee. Instead of asking the boys and girls to spell the words, you have them give definitions. Announce this competition in advance, allowing the pupils time to study for it. Keep a list of the two winners—the best performances by a boy and by a girl—and add to it at the end of each month. Then, for the culmination, offer prizes to the "Best Definers." Incidentally, we suggest a boy *and* girl, rather than the two students who lead the group, because almost invariably the girls will win. By this device, we are able to avoid boring the boys, causing them to withdraw. Check to be sure your school district permits rewards.

TEACHING READING SKILLS
IN ALL SUBJECT AREAS

Duplicate your own materials

For the teaching of reading skills, we believe you should prepare your own materials. You may use magazines, newspapers, or textbooks as sources, or you may compose your own text. This material, however, should be reproduced and distributed to your students; use carbon copies, mimeographed sheets, or even photostated pages. These may then be included in the children's notebooks. They may write on them directly, do the exercises on them, and retain them for study and review. You are, in effect, making an individualized workbook—giving pupils on different levels of ability, varying reading materials—even though you are teaching the same basic skill to all of them. By preparing your own materials (and these may be used for more than one or two classes, and reused year after year) you are able to select topics of interest which will, in and of themselves, serve as motivation. You may decide on a short story—"Cemetery Path" is one of our favorites—or an article, a book jacket excerpt, or a human interest story. Even a book review, or a "Letter to the Editor" might prove interesting. The sources are, truly, endless. As you train yourself in this type of teaching, you will find materials which will enable you to teach any reading skill while, at the same time, covering your subject area.

Using contextual clues to learn the meanings of new words

1. Using material which you have selected, duplicate and distribute to your students, list on the board those words which are to be studied. Explain to the pupils that very often they will encounter material which contains "clues" to the definitions of words which are strange to them.

2. Instruct your pupils to find the first new word listed on the board in the text, and to read, silently, the entire sentence in which it is found. Ask for a volunteer to read that sentence aloud, and then request a possible definition from the class. Then have the next sentence read aloud. Discuss the definitions offered, and when the class agrees, have the definition written on the board. Bring out the fact that the students were able to figure out the meaning of the word from the context. Then list the clues the boys and girls may look for.

a) Often an author will use a word, and follow with a definition immediately after it: What is *oxygen?*

> *Oxygen,* a colorless, odorless gas makes up approximately one-fifth of the earth's atmosphere. It is, however, far more important what that figure indicates, for it is the gas which sustains all living things. Without it we would immediately die. Our brain cells, for example, cannot live without oxygen for even one minute.

b) Many times you will find a word defined in the sentence following the one in which it is used: Define *pub*.

Pubs are found in all parts of England. A pub is really a cross between a bar and a living room. It functions as both. Pubs have wonderful names, such as "Sherlock Holmes," or the "Bull and the Bear." They serve many Englishmen as their homes away from home, where they amuse themselves, chatting, having an ale or playing darts. Television is very much in evidence in many pubs today, the contribution of the twentieth century.

c) The definition may not be stated, but you are able to determine what it is by carefully reading the paragraph containing the word. What is the meaning of *hypothesis?*

The *hypothesis* offered by Albert Einstein, which we have heard called "relativity," contains the idea that there are not three, but four dimensions. We are familiar with length, width and height, but Einstein added to these a fourth dimension, time.

After your pupils have listed the new words in their notebooks, follow the method outlined in the previous section, for implanting them in the students' memories. It must be stressed, many times, that review is necessary to retain words. Even as adults we don't learn new vocabulary easily. Try this experiment: Here is a list of words, and their definitions, taken from the dictionary. Memorize them, but do not review them often during the following month. Test yourself at the end of 30 days. You may then wish to try the "Use, Repeat, Review" method, to see if it will be of assistance to you personally.

Bombast—high sounding, inflated.

Excrescence—immoderate or abnormal outgrowth or enlargement.

Glyptodon—large, extinct mammal related to the armadillo.

Matelote—stew of fish and wine sauce.

Olio—a medley.

Panoply—a suit of armor, or a covering.

Protean—assuming different forms.

Puissant—potent.

Sciolism—pretension to scholarship.

Vitiate—to poison or taint.

Selection of the main idea of a paragraph

Selecting the main idea of a paragraph is another of the reading skills which may be taught in any subject area.

Choose material from text, magazine or newspaper. Have your pupils read the paragraph. Then request them to write notes to their best friends telling what this paragraph is about—in one sentence. In other words, what you are doing is helping the pupil to select the basic idea, omitting the explanations or the frills. You may choose to phrase this in this manner: "If this paragraph were in a newspaper, what do you think the headline would be? What would the 'lead-off' sentence contain?" Point out that often, but certainly not always, the main idea is found in the first sentence of the paragraph. It is like peeping through a keyhole to get a glimpse of the room inside. Then use this variation: List several headlines, and have pupils select the best one—and give their reasons for having selected it. There are a series of rules you may wish to give to your students to help them select this main idea:

1. Read the entire paragraph.
2. Get an idea of its meaning—what is said—in the pupil's own words.
3. Select a headline or title for the paragraph.
4. Prove that this is correct by selecting items from the paragraph relating to it.

For example, here is a sample paragraph:

When one travels, one sees many aspects of life in other lands, and while people in strange countries live basically the same way we do, there are many differences. In some warm countries, for example, people close their businesses and take an afternoon nap after lunch. This custom, in Spain, is called the "siesta." Dinner hour, too, varies, getting later as you approach the equator. Dinner in Italy is usually served at about nine in the evening, and in Spain even later. People in hot climates seem to hate the sun. In Puerto Rico, for instance, ladies will never allow themselves to get a suntan. They protect themselves with umbrellas, if, for some reason, they must be out of doors while the sun is strong. In colder climes, such as Scandinavia, swimming in temperatures of 40° Fahrenheit is not unusal. We would be very uncomfortable, if we were to try that.

You might ask your pupils to state what they consider to be the main idea of this paragraph. Or, you might have them select a title from the following:

A. The Siesta.
B. Dinner Time in Italy.
C. Life in Other Lands.
D. Swimming in Scandinavia.

This skill is used, very often, in standardized reading tests; it is the reading comprehension part of the examination. (Often the only other part included is a section on vocabulary.) Both skills may be taught. It is essential that your students' work be checked very carefully to show them their errors—and to try to determine how and why they made them. This checking may be done by the students themselves, and by other students. Occasionally it should be done by you.

Reading and thinking critically

In a word association game, if someone said "fact," what word would you say? Probably "fiction." But surprisingly, it is more important for us to teach our children to separate fact from opinion—to think critically of what they read or hear. How can we do this? Try the following method:

Have your pupils read a number of short paragraphs, such as the following:

a. We anticipate the rain in Spain will stay mainly in the plains. This has been the annual rainfall pattern in Spain for many years, and, although there have been variations in the amount, and in the specific place, we believe these climate conditions will continue.

b. There will probably be a woman president elected in the United States before the year 2068. As women become a more important part of the population because of their functions as wives and mothers, they will become more powerful, and more influential. As they are freed from their household chores, more and more of them will enter politics, and, as a natural outgrowth of this, we will probably see a Madam President within the next hundred years.

c. The population of the entire world is growing at an astounding rate. By the middle of the year 1967 it had exceeded three billion by four-hundred million. In November, 1967, it was announced by the Bureau of the Census, of the United States Government, that our nation had more than two hundred million people. One out of approximately seventeen people living on the earth is American—or, to be more specific, a United Statesian.

d. It has been observed that the world is now in a state of constant change. Our appearance is changing, in terms of styles of hair, clothing, and manner. The possibility exists that there may be genetic changes, as well. If a large proportion of our populations resorts to the use of the hallucinatory producing drugs, and if their units of heredity, the genes, are affected, a new, even startling type of human being might arise. He may have developed from genes which would cause him to have one eye and two noses. Are we willing to risk such changes?

After having your students study these selections, question them. What devices are used, in these paragraphs, to show that items a, b, and d are opinion, and only c is fact. Have them list for you these clues:

1. We anticipate. . . .
2. There will probably be. . . .

    3. The possibility exists that. . . .
    4. The . . . claims. . . .
    5. It is believed that. . . .
    6. It is rumored that. . . .
    7. . . . thinks that. . . .

Bring out the concept that the presences of these expressions indicate the material is opinion rather than fact. Point out that all too often we overlook these very important words. Other terms, used very frequently, particularly in news reports, are worth noting:

    8. High sources report. . . .
    9. Informed sources tell us. . . .

These are both within the realm of possibility, but are not necessarily factual.

You may give an exercise such as the following:

LABEL EACH OF THE SENTENCES "FACT" OR "OPINION."

1. Senator Jones believes he has a good chance of being elected to the presidency of the United Kingdom.
2. He has had many years of experience serving as dog catcher of his native state.
3. It is rumored that if he is elected he will put a turkey in every oven—whether you like turkey or not.
4. His office anticipates he will carry the states of New California, Old Jersey and Florakota.
5. His large family will be campaigning for him, in addition to the large staff he has hired.

We have used these examples to inject humor into a classic classroom situation. Should you chose to do so, be sure it does not detract from the concept you are teaching. Select materials of interest to your students, which are within the range of their comprehension, or their experiences. Too often we use materials which are uninteresting, and to which boys and girls are more or less indifferent. You will find they will learn far more if you make their lessons games, their exercises fun.

Summarizing any reading material

Have you ever closed a book and asked yourself, "What was that all about?" In the case of children, this is true even more often, and particularly so with our slow learners. The lesson which follows is an invaluable one, and may be used in any subject, with the possible exception of mathematics.

You may wish to announce to your class, "I am going to teach you a very simple way to summarize everything or anything you read, and remember it as well. It's called the 'Five W's.' What words come to your mind that begin with the letter W?" Elicit from them the following:

1. Who?
2. When?
3. Where?
4. What?
5. Why?

Items *one, two* and *three* are obvious, in their connection with writing a summary. Item four is then elaborated to cover what was said about the subject (the "who"), and item five is enlarged to ask "Why was this material written?"

You may choose to utilize this manner of questioning to have the class write simple book reports. Or, in assigning a chapter of a textbook, you have but to say, "Answer the Five W's for homework," and you know that the student will have to think about the chapter, and not give you rote answers directly from the text. Every so often you should carefully review their responses, particularly to items four and five, to be sure they are answering intelligently. They may need your assistance, too, in selecting the most important points, but they will learn, from such exercises, just how to do so.

Reading and following printed directions

No matter how little or how much education one has, he still will have to read and follow printed instructions often. The house-wife follows recipes, her husband puts together toys, furniture, or other items sold in an unassembled state, her son plays games such as Password or Monopoly, and her daughter sews a dress. All of these activities, and a host of others, require the ability to read instructions and interpret them. Should we not teach this skill to our pupils, and make sure they fully understand it?

To motivate your pupils, you may wish to use the "Instruction Test." This test requires the student to read through the printed instructions from beginning to end, and will promote gaiety as well. While it may be familiar to you, most children, we have found, have never seen it before.

CAN YOU FOLLOW INSTRUCTIONS?

1. Write your name in the upper left hand corner of this page.
2. Write the date in the upper right hand corner of the page.
3. If you are a male, write the word "male" in the lower right hand corner.
4. If you are a female, write the word "female" in the lower right hand corner.
5. Read every step before you do anything else.
6. Add the following numbers: 33, 44, 55, 66, 77.
7. Call out your answer in a loud voice.
8. Think of the smallest number you can which is divisible by thirteen.
9. Call out that number in a loud voice.
10. In the space below, draw a circle, a square and a triangle.

11. Place your pencil or pen through the center of the circle. If your circle was not large enough, draw another one.

12. Multiply two hundred thousand two by four hundred thousand four.

13. Call out your answer.
14. Now announce, loud and clear, "I have almost finished."
15. Divide the sum of six hundred nine thousand by twelve.
16. Call out this answer. Then shout, "I have finished."
17. If you have read this entire page, omit steps six through sixteen.
18. Write the words, "The End" below.

After the class has completed this test, distribute a legitimate series of instructions, such as the following:

What simple test can the chemist do to determine the presence of an acid?

The simplest method the chemist uses to test for the presence of an acid utilizes litmus paper, prepared commercially in pieces ½" wide by 2" long. Strips of both blue and red litmus paper are needed to perform accurate tests.

If water is touched to either red or blue litmus paper, there is no color change. If an acid is touched to them, the red will remain red, but the blue will change to red immediately. Therefore, using these simple strips of litmus, we are able to determine easily the presence of an acid. The strips may be used only one time, because the chemical they contain, called litmus, is changed permanently when touched by an acid and cannot react again.

After your students have read this entire set of instructions, do the following:

1. Review the new vocabulary, defining the unfamiliar words carefully.

2. Have the pupils carefully state the specific problem they are solving: Testing for the presence of an acid.

3. Have them outline the actual steps they will do in performing the test.

4. Elicit from the students what, specifically, they will have accomplished by performing this test.

When this work has been completed, have the students work up a list of instructions for some activity with which they are familiar. It might be to bake a cake, play a game or travel somewhere. Place a list of suggestions on the board so that each child may choose one.

Readings for safety and for health! Interpreting signs and labels

Can you imagine how hazardous it is to go through life without being able to read and interpret the word "Danger." There are, unquestionably, many foreign born citizens who cannot read that word, or many other words or phrases which are so important to their well-being—the signs in the streets, in the subways, on the highways. Nor can they read the labels pasted on bottles or cans they bring home, which may contain poisonous ingredients. There are probably youngsters in our schools today who would fall into the same category—who also are unable to read even these very vital words.

In working with slow learners, here are some words which they must learn and understand. Their very survival may depend on this:

Danger	STOP	Hospital	Police	POISON
POLICE STATION		Walk	DO NOT WALK	Fire
FIRE DEPARTMENT		Emergency	EMERGENCY ROOM	
Exit	DANGEROUS CROSSING		Curve	ENTRANCE
Emergency Exit		SLOW	School	

No doubt you will think of other words to add to this list. We are getting down to the very basics of life, and you are familiar with the lives of your children.

How shall you teach these words?

1. Print them on oaktag sheets, about one foot square. Refer to them as "Survival Words."

2. Explain each word carefully. *Elicit from the children* why they need to know the particular word. Such stories as "I had to take my little brother to the hospital, and we needed to find the Emergency Room in a hurry" are good. Dramatize the situations.

3. Decorate your room with the words, and with other signs, showing them in context. (The highway signs for curve, for example.)

4. Review the words periodically. Use any drills you find successful, but be sure each child has mastered these survival words.

5. As a homework assignment, have the children teach the survival words to the other members of their families, if necessary.

The labels on many household items are extremely important too. Have your pupils bring in some of these labels, or copies of them. If you wish to show the actual can or bottle, remove the contents, if dangerous, before bringing it into the classroom. Household ammonia and lye are excellent examples.

It is also appropriate to have your pupils read the warning in regard to smoking which is to be found on every package of cigarettes.

Using the parts of a book efficiently

This skill can save your children many hours of work. It is useful to use their own texts for this exercise:

Review the following parts. Ask them to tell you what information they will find. Then add any they have omitted.

1. Title page—gives title, author, publisher and date.

What does this actually tell us? The title suggests to us what we may find in the book. The author and publisher enable us to locate a copy of any book—from the library, for example. The copyright date tells us the approximate date of publication.

2. The table of contents.

   A list of the names of the broad topics or units, usually in the form of chapters.

3. The index.

   Usually located at the end of the book, the index lists every subject discussed in the book.

4. If the text has a glossary, have the pupils turn to it, and identify what it is, and how it differs from a dictionary. Point out that not all texts have glossaries.

Utilize the text to become familiar with the parts of a book, and extend this to include the youngsters' other texts.

For all skills

Whenever you teach any skill, remember that it must be repeated, reiterated, and reinforced. The more review and drill you are able to include, the better; but be sure you do not bore your students. When they have mastered something, proceed to the next item. By belaboring a concept, often the children lose interest and you will find it far harder to motivate them. Above all, make your drill work fun to do. It is as easy to give an assignment with humor or drama in it as it is to give a dull one. In your own reading, when you come across something which you find will be useful, clip it out and save it. This sort of library is particularly valuable when you make up your lesson plans.

Now! Let's get them to read

If you want to get your pupils to read, here are some suggestions. If they seem very obvious to you, please forgive the approach we are using, but we have discovered that, even though these methods seem ridiculously fundamental, they are not in general use.

Assign at least five book reports a year. This includes every subject, major or minor, with the exception of Health Education, and even in this area there are books available.

Many pupils don't read unless they have to. Once the habit is formed, or they find they enjoy books, this may change. For this reason we suggest a report every six weeks.

Give a stated form for the report. This may be the "Five W's" or any other, but let the children know exactly what is expected of them. Here are some for you to consider:

1. What are three things you learned from this book?
2. Why do you think things happened, in the book, in the way in which they did?
3. What did you learn about the times in which this book took place?
4. In what ways can you use three of the things you read about?
5. How will mankind benefit from some of the things you read about?
6. Would you want to read more about this subject, and if so, where could you find more material?

You may wish to substitute for reports:

Charts	Plays
Dioramas	Poems

To encourage reading:

1. Take your students on visits to libraries available to them—both in school, and outside.
2. Help them to select books while they are in the library. Make recommendations.

Accept long essays from such magazines as *Life, Look, National Geographic,* and *Sports Illustrated.*

SUMMARY

The methods we have outlined for improvement of reading may be used singly or in conjunction with one another. You may discover your classes are not lacking in all of these skills, but there is no class which will not benefit from some of them. Since reading is so basic to all learning, children who are unable to grasp information from the printed page feel defeated before they even enter school. As you use these methods, and a youngster achieves success, point out his achievements to him. By reviewing his mimeographed exercises, he is able to see his progress from skill to skill. You are thus able to teach subject matter and reading, and to build a child's self-image—all simultaneously. Don't you agree this is a tremendous bargain—three for the price of one?

By teaching reading in science class, or in mathematics, in social studies, or even in foreign language, in hygiene or industrial arts, in music or art you are helping the children improve the skills they need more than any others, both in school and in daily living. Building word knowledge by using a technique involving multiple choice questions, as we outlined, serves several purposes. The child learns the meanings of many new words, per se, and also gets practice in working with exercises which directly prepare him for the majority of standardized reading tests. You are teaching your pupils vocabulary, and simultaneously teaching them to take these tests. The same is true when you teach the skill called "Selecting the main idea of a paragraph." On the tests, this is often the section called, "Select the sentence or phrase which is the best title for this paragraph." Certainly when a child is able to do this, he comprehends what he is reading.

"Using contextual clues to learn the meanings of new words" is a valuable technique for the child to know because it is applicable to the reading of newspapers and magazines, as well as textbooks. "Using the parts of a book efficiently," "Reading and thinking critically," "Summarizing," "The ability to read and follow instructions," are all important tools which our slow learners need. "Reading signs and labels" should be the concern of every teacher, for without being overly dramatic, these may involve matters of life and death. By utilizing the success building program, you may change the child's self-image—he realizes he can do well on tests, instead of poorly. His feelings of defeat may change, and, if you are truly successful, his entire pattern of learning may be improved.

6

using social studies
to stimulate the interest
of the slow learner

To teach social studies successfully to slow learners involves teaching subject matter—history, geography and current events; but more important it includes the teaching of social skills—of living and working together. To teach the latter, we use committees to do research, carry on construction work, have debates and panel discussions, perform playlets and charades, play games and take trips. Each of these activities is important in terms of the social development of the slow learner, who learns so much more readily from experiences than in other ways.

In teaching the subject matter or current events, we have tried to create interest by using folk music and novels to teach social conditions; by choosing controversial subjects for debates and panel discussions; by games such as "Twenty Questions." We suggest you use a cultural immersion program to teach geography, and to stimulate the slow learner. Other techniques you might wish to experiment with are: utilizing biographies to make famous individuals seem to be alive; creating a school or class social studies newspaper. We include sources for easily obtained materials with which to teach Negro history, and have also mentioned the use of magazines, and other similar publications for their motivational value. We offer relatively simple devices to structure situations in which children must work together: reading, writing, doing units on occupations, and preparing committee scrapbooks and encyclopedias.

By utilizing some or all of these methods, you will add vitality and interest to your social studies classes, and encourage the development of good social relationships between members of the class.

LIVING AND WORKING HARMONIOUSLY

Implicit in the teaching of social studies is instruction in social behavior, in the art of living and working harmoniously with other people. It is most important that this be included in the course, along with the geography, history and current events, found in the curriculum. Certainly we must try to teach living cooperatively in every subject, but while we may fail to do this in others, we should surely try to include it in this area. How do we teach boys and girls to cooperate with one another, to enjoy working in groups? Lecturing won't do. We just can't say, "Do as I say, and not as I do." The children must be put into structured situations, where they have common goals, and strive to achieve these. Children can determine a hypocrite quite quickly and have little respect for the individual after that.

Committee work is an excellent means of accomplishing this. You may decide to set up any or all of a variety of such committees—to do research, to debate, to build dioramas, even to discuss the material being studied in class. When you establish committees, include instructions for rotating the leadership, giving every child, including the slow learner, the opportunity to "chair" the group. You may decide to have different tasks done by each committee. In that case, try to suit the task to the particular children. For example, in a unit on the United Nations, one group might work on collecting pictures of inhabitants of various nations, another might make drawings and paintings, a third group could learn songs, a fourth dances, and a fifth group might prepare a dinner of foods of the various nations. In this way children are learning subject matter, and experiencing the most important lesson of working together.

TEACHING SOCIAL CONDITIONS THROUGH MUSIC

Can't we teach social conditions throughout the world through music? The folk singers of today, like the minstrels of yore, have long chronicled the ills of society. Utilizing their efforts, we are able to teach our young people some of the problems the world has faced, and is facing today. The slow learner is attracted to this because it is a form of entertainment as well as a teaching tool. Play the record of the Weavers singing "So Long, It's Been Good to Know You," and the dust bowl becomes a real place. Try playing Ed McCurdy's marvelous record "Songs and Stories of the Civil War"—the music is excellent, and the entire performance memorable as well as educational. Negro singers have long been seeking to call attention to the problems their people face.

Using such recordings in class guarantees the attention and interest of the children, but you must review the recording first to be sure it is worthy of your selection.

PANEL DISCUSSIONS, DEBATES AND "TOWN HALL" TYPE MEETINGS

Walking through the hall one morning, we observed a scene causing us to walk into the room to hear what was going on. The children were sitting almost at the edges of their seats. Almost all of their hands were raised; some looked as if they were about to burst. At the front of the room the chairman called for order several times. Finally, they settled down to what was a most exciting lesson. It was a "Town Hall" type of meeting, on the topic "Old enough to fight, old enough to vote."

Panel discussions, and debates too, are most effective devices for "waking up the sleepy heads," and for stimulating the slow learner to think. However, each child must become involved, must take part.

Choose stimulating subjects. For example, children never tire of the "eighteen-year-old vote" issue.

In election years, "Why I support the candidate of my choice" can cause heated debates, which is, of course, one of your objectives. Other possible topics:

What the United States means to me.
How do you, the younger generation, feel about . . . . ?
(*This might be smoking, drinking, dating, homework, movies, censorship.*)

One law I believe should be repealed or changed is
. . . .

A new law we should suggest is . . . .

My favorite magazine is . . . . because . . . . (*or news-paper, television show, performer, movie, politician*).

Choice of topic is extremely important, and you will find that if your class makes the selection, it will probably be far more enthused than if you assign it.

Allow children to carry on the programs. Train them to do this—and then you are able to sit back and enjoy them yourself.

GUESSING GAMES—"TWENTY QUESTIONS," FOR EXAMPLE

Every once in a while, try guessing games, because they offer a change of pace, which is often just what is needed to get or keep the children interested. Encourage your children to think of interesting subjects, and have them consult with you about them. When you feel a particularly good one is suggested, allow time for it at the end of a period, or during the part of the day set aside for relaxation.

To play this game, one person, who knows the identity of the hidden personality, stands at the front of the room. The others question him; he may answer only "Yes" or "No." The object is to identify the individual before twenty questions are asked. Choosing personalities with unusual occupations make the games the most interesting. Astronauts and explorers are quite challenging, as are settlers such as Brigham Young. You may use this game, too, to motivate a lesson. You may wish to help your slow learner by reviewing in advance all of the facts dealing with the personality assigned to him.

CONSTRUCTION PROJECTS

Although it is many years, I vividly recall saying to a child, "Why, Bill, I never knew you could do such beautiful work!" Bill had constructed a magnificent replica of an Elizabethan Theatre. Some slow learners need to gain in self-esteem and in self-worth. If they are talented in drawing or in carpentry, have them construct dioramas; these are best done as committee projects. The children may use cardboard boxes to house the scenes; plastic figures are available which are inexpensive and realistic.

Before the diorama is made, have the children do research to determine what they should include, and to be sure they are historically and geographically accurate. Museums have beautiful samples on exhibit, and you may wish to show them to your children, to give them ideas. Of course, instruct them in techniques —and tell them that you do not expect their work to be as good, but, nevertheless, it must be as accurate as they can make it.

Bill's theatre is ten years old—and still it inspires other children.

USE BOOKS TO GIVE YOUR SLOW LEARNERS A TRUE PICTURE OF LIFE DURING OTHER TIMES, OR IN OTHER PLACES

One of the finest books ever written, we believe, is John Steinbeck's *Grapes of Wrath*. Reading this gives our children an experience they probably will never forget. Nor will they forget the problems of the period.

Howard Fast presents the critical viewpoint in regard to the United States. Nevertheless his books, such as *Citizen Tom Paine* or *The Vanishing American*, can be read by your classes, and discussed with great value.

If you are teaching a unit on Hawaii, what could be better than suggesting to your classes they read portions of James Michener's wonderful book *Hawaii?* (They might also be encouraged to see "South Pacific," the play and film made from it.) *The Source*, also written by Michener, makes the Holy Land come to life.

Non-fiction, too, can be a means of transplanting our children to other times. *Guadalcanal Diary* might be assigned to classes studying World War II. The list of appropriate books is endless. Biographical works, too, are both stimulating and enjoyable. We have found the boys and girls love them, and often identify with the heroic characters depicted. For example, the study of the life of Dr. Martin Luther King, or John or Robert Kennedy would be of great value. Our children do not read as many books as they should; by careful selection on your part, and by recommendations based on your knowledge of the child's ability, you can teach him history and develop his reading comprehension and vocabulary. Give him books he will enjoy. The slow learner may start reading for pleasure—a condition to be devoutly desired. A discussion with your school or public librarian in this regard might prove very worthwhile. Having samples of books which fit the children's needs, and arranging to have the children borrow them from the classroom instead of the library, will encourage reading, and will enrich the children.

TOTAL IMMERSION GEOGRAPHY

What did you do in school today, dear?

We had so much fun today, Mommy. We learned a French song, and we ate a little piece of cheese pie. It's too bad we aren't older—because the teacher said if we were, she'd have given us wine to go with it.

Do you think I can join your class tomorrow?

To teach geography effectively (Illustration 6-1), try the total immersion approach, an all-out effort to teach the culture of the nation. For example, get records of the music of the land; pictures of the costumes worn; slides or films of the cities and open spaces; art, and handicrafts; samples of food typical of the meals eaten by the native population. You may wish to have the children make scrapbooks—an activity which is particularly beneficial to the slow learners. They may write to embassies or consulates for information and materials. This gives them valuable experience in writing business letters, and they have the pleasure of looking forward to receiving mail, which boys and girls usually enjoy. They may also visit travel agencies, museums, and used book shops, where they can try to find old copies of *National Geographic*. Treated as if this were a treasure hunt, it becomes a really pleasurable experience for the slow learner. Recipes, architecture of the land, customs, idiosyncrasies of the inhabitants, all add interest, and a sense of closeness to the people being studied. For example, why do Indian women wear a mark, resembling a beauty mark, on their foreheads? Why are the Hawaiians descended from so many different nationalities? Why

Illustration 6-1

do the English drink warm beer? Who was the King known as "crazy Ludwig"? Injecting such material adds immeasurably to everyone's enjoyment of the study.

Committees should be set up to do research, and report their findings. Use each child's talents, and try to help him to develop new ones. As a pièce de résistance, add some vocabulary in the language of the land. It need not be a great deal, but greetings, numbers, and perhaps a short conversation will give your children bonuses, and items of interest to discuss with their families. The slow learner can easily be helped to excel in this, if you spend a bit of time tutoring him.

EXPLORING YOUR CITY WITH YOUR CHILDREN

Overheard on Times Square

GREYHOUND BUS TOUR DIRECTOR: "Tour, lady? Trip around Manhattan. See all the sights—Chinatown, the Bowery, Grant's Tomb. . . ."

"No thanks. I live here."

"But, have you seen all these spots?"

"Don't be ridiculous! Of course I haven't! They're just for tourists."

So often people are really unfamiliar with their own cities. This is probably more true of individuals living in a metropolis than in a small town. However, by finding the time to explore the older parts of the city with your class, you can point out the architecture, the historical sights, the food markets, the parks and the museums. You develop an enjoyment of your immediate surroundings. Then search out the newer areas, determining what will be of interest to boys and girls. Ferret out sources of inexpensive and free entertainment which are available to your children, and give this information to them or have them gather it themselves. The knowledge of the locations of parks, playgrounds, libraries, theatres, tennis courts, and other places for spending leisure time profitably, will be of value both to the children and to their families.

ESTABLISH A SOCIAL STUDIES NEWSPAPER— ON A CLASS OR SCHOOL BASIS

Have children write articles for a newspaper—as if they were alive during a different period of time. For example, "Columbus Discovers America," "Ponce de Leon Seeks Fountain of Youth," or "Atlantic Ocean Turns into Tea."

These topics may be handled truthfully, or they may be covered "tongue-in-cheek." If you use an article on Columbus, the date of the paper would be 1492, and might include sports, fashions, recipes and even a comic strip of the times.

Assign committees to prepare the various sections of the newspaper, so that all of the children gain the benefits of working together. Assign to the slow learner topics which he can handle. Help him, when necessary, to write his article or structure the committee he is in to insure helpful co-workers. If possible, have the children do the actual duplicating of the material, the collating, and the stapling. All of these activities require their working together.

THE HISTORY OF MINORITY GROUPS IN THE UNITED STATES

This topic must not be neglected, for it is badly needed by every person being educated in our schools. In the era in which we live, every child needs some knowledge of the total development of our society. For materials to teach Negro history, you may wish to write to:

Library, Ebony Magazine
1820 South Michigan Avenue
Chicago, Illinois 62521

Request the teaching kits of pictures showing distinguished Negroes who have made outstanding contributions to history. Negro students need to learn this information, but other children need it even more. *Life* magazine, too, has published a great deal of valuable material—including many pictures for creating excellent bulletin board displays.

MAKE NATIONAL, STATE, AND LOCAL ELECTIONS EXCITING!

In the years before the American Revolution, one of the slogans heard around the nation was later incorporated into a famous document; the words were "All men are created equal." From 1775 until 1781, some of most frequently spoken were "We must hang together." In the campaign of 1828, it was, "Every man is as good as his neighbor." During Reconstruction, Lincoln's immortal phrase "With malice toward none," was to be found in all of the publications of the time. Other frequently heard words were "Let us have peace." In 1928 people spoke of the "Chicken in every pot." In 1932 it was "The forgotten man." In 1939, referring to old age pensions, the newspapers wrote of "Thirty dollars every Thursday."

In any election year, create an interest in the elections being held. We have found the study of slogans to be an excellent motivational device.

Stir up as much enthusiasm as you are able to. With debates, be careful to present the views of all of the major candidates, stressing an understanding of the issues. Have the children analyze the campaigns; utilize the newspapers and news magazines to check for facts and for editorializing in the news columns. Should you wish to invite speakers to address the children, the League of Women Voters has an excellent Speakers Bureau for this purpose, and they also have fine printed materials which they distribute. Your slow learners may be involved in polling the children in their class or in the entire school to add further interest in the campaigns. These may be published in the social studies newspapers. The slow learners must be made to feel an interest in politics and government, so that when they become adults, they will be able to vote intelligently.

VIGNETTES

One July day in 1804, in Weehawken, New Jersey two men met to settle their differences in a duel. One was the Vice President of the United States. The other was the man who, he felt, had prevented him from becoming President. Of course there were different accounts of what took place; Alexander Hamilton, Senator from New York, leveled his pistol and appeared to take careful aim. But, when the shot rang out, it was Hamilton who fell, mortally wounded. The Vice President, Aaron Burr, had killed him.

Probably the most interesting subject in the world is people. Why do we, as adults, gossip? Why do we read the columnists so avidly? Why are the escapades of the movie stars front-page news? And, above all, how can we make use of this interest in people in our classes? One way is by using "vignettes," stories about people. If, in our teaching, we incorporate such stories, our children are interested and enthused. People haven't changed very much in hundreds of years—witness Cleopatra, Caesar, and Marc Anthony. Telling their story to young people makes them human beings faced with problems. Colorful personalities in history, like Abraham Lincoln or John Kennedy, make the subject fascinating.

You may also find eyewitness accounts of various events in history, and have these read to your classes. Newspapers or letters written at the time add interesting details. The point is to treat the great of the world as people, and not as statues in the Hall of Fame.

LEAVING LEGACIES TO THE SCHOOL

You may use this concept as motivation—namely, that the work the children do will live after them, that as long as you teach you will have it on display. Then explain what you are requesting the children to do. They, as committees, are to make either encyclopedias or scrapbooks of current events or of topics they are studying. They may use magazine articles from *Look, Life* or *National Geographic,* and newspaper articles. After each article is pasted on construction paper, a short summary is written by the child below it. These pages are then bound into large books.

This is an exceptionally good method to use with slow learners. It encourages them to search for materials, and to read and summarize them. They can easily achieve success with this activity. You may teach them to read the topic sentence of each paragraph carefully in preparing their summaries. We suggest you give credit for this work as part of their grades. Encourage them to decorate their books, to add drawings, and to make a beautiful finished product which may then be displayed, and kept on display for years to come.

When forming the committees, place the slow learners with children who will willingly assist them. Allow the committee to select its own topic. When the books are completed, they should be titled, "Current Events of 1968, compiled by class 5-311. The committee consisted of Jane Jones, Mary Smith, etc." You may wish to invite the principal of the school to see the work the committees have produced. Encourage each child to be as creative as he knows how to be. Poems, paintings, montages may all be included.

OCCUPATIONS

What is more important than the choice of an occupation? This topic should be taught in every subject area, but it is particularly significant in social studies.

Ask the children which fields of endeavor interest them. List these on the board, and then divide the class into committees which will be studying related occupations. This may be done with third or fourth graders, and certainly with any group older than that.

We feel that interviewing is one of the best techniques for studying occupations, and that it helps children to develop poise and self-assurance. Have your class develop with you a series of guiding questions. Elicit them from the group, but be sure they are similar to the following:

1. Do you like your work? Why?
2. What do you do during your working day?
3. How did you prepare for this work?
4. How can you advance in your job?
5. Would you recommend it to someone still in school? Why?

Mimeograph this list of questions. Give each child as many forms as he has people to interview. Have the children ask the questions, and fill in the forms while they are doing the actual interview.

Have the committees report on their findings. Your slow learners will be able to do the interviewing, but may need help in the reporting aspect of the work. However, you may request written or oral reports, or a combination of both.

SUMMARY

To teach social studies effectively, we must encompass two areas: we must cover subject matter—history, geography and current events—and we must train our children in the art of living and working with other people. A variety of techniques have been suggested which will enable you to teach these simultaneously.

They are specially geared to the slow learner. Group work, panel discussions, debates, construction projects, exploring your city, publishing a class newspaper, and preparing scrapbooks all will help you to reach both goals, and as an added bonus heighten the children's interest in your subject.

Included, too, to stimulate thought, are an assortment of other strategies. Many young people have a great interest in folk music; you can use this medium to teach them social conditions. Review work can be transformed into fun by virtue of converting it into games—and any sort of quiz, when called a "Guessing Game," is greeted entirely differently by your children than if it is labeled "Test" or "Examination." Firsthand knowledge, achieved by communicating directly with people in societies or lands other than one's own, is another valuable method. We suggest too that you use an approach we call "Total Immersion Geography."

By introducing economics to our slow learners, we help to educate them in this important aspect of living. We should make our boys and girls aware, too, and excited about elections and campaigns.

We hope you will consider using fiction to teach history, and adding fillips to make it fascinating by drawing vignettes of famous people. You will, we are sure, also include some study of the background of minority groups, which is so necessary in the modern world. And so, too, is a study of occupations, which can be one of great significance to your children.

Your slow learner needs to learn geography; but he needs to learn to feel confidence in himself more. Give him projects and activities in which he can be successful. Stimulate him to think, get him interested in history, and you enlarge his horizons permanently. Above all, by helping him to work well with others, by structuring many situations where he is forced to do so, you equip him for employment and for life.

7

successful strategies for teaching science to slow learners

To teach science successfully to slow learners, we have one tremendous asset with which to work—children love doing experiments. It is relatively simple to make most of the learning in this subject experiential. Demonstrations are a good substitute when experimentation by the children is not possible. From these activities we are able to teach the children to make observations and to draw conclusions from these observations. We can then extend these results to concepts (Illustration 7-1). We will discuss these and other methods for giving the children as many experiences as possible.

Encourage your children to bring in objects of scientific interest, for it is with this material that we can build understanding of scientific phenomena. Pursue topics which capture the children's interests—the Loch Ness monster, perhaps, or UFO's (Unidentified Flying Objects). Such topics are often found in newspapers or magazines. Always have attention-getting objects on display in your classroom. Use audio-visual equipment as often as you can—microscopes, bioscopes, films, filmstrip or overhead projectors. When there are funds to purchase specimens, it is very effective to have the children do dissections of frogs, white mice, fetal pigs, or other laboratory specimens, all lifeless and preserved of course. Help those children who are interested in doing so to make collections of rocks, seeds, flowers, leaves or shells. Assist the child who wishes to construct models or devices such as crystal radios.

Illustration 7-1

The geological history of the area in which you live provides another interesting tangent. The study of astronomy, and the discussion of astrology will fascinate your slow learner and his classmates too. Surely the space program of both the United States and Russia is worthy of time and attention. When teaching natural phenomena, use slides or photographs. Because our children are consumers now, and very soon will deal with even larger amounts of money, work on intelligent buying is worthwhile. There are certain scientific truths which are vital to the survival of every human being. We must be very sure that our slow learners master these. For example, the proper ways to deal with electricity in the home should be taught in every grade. Every science class should devote some time to the study of smoking cigarettes, so that our students become extremely familiar with its possible dangers. Narcotics, too, must be discussed, if we are to truly prepare our children for today's world. Setting up a school or class museum will add to the enjoyment of the subject by our slow learners. Because doctors are adamant in regard to the effects of overweight, it behooves us to teach our children about calories, diet and even exercise. Lastly we suggest you give your slow learners an understanding of heart and other organ transplants, which we believe will become more and more frequent and important as time progresses.

SUGGESTIONS

Experiments

Without question, the best way to teach science to slow learners is through experiments. It is also the most enjoyable, the most effective and the most motivating. Children love to work with chemicals, to dissect, to do all of the various things which compose the science curricula. This method of teaching is excellent because it enables each child to participate actively in each lesson. He is not a bystander, he is a doer. The slow learner is neither hampered by the fact that he cannot read very well, nor by the fact that he does not grasp concepts too quickly. The teacher is easily able to guide him from one thought to another.

Each experiment should be done with a purpose. The most frequently used phraseology is "What are we trying to find out?" Or it might be, "What problem are we trying to solve?" Then, as the children perform the experiment, we must help them to make observations and, by skillful questions, teach them how to draw conclusions. Keep this basic plan in mind as you plan your work.

If you are able to schedule an experiment each day, you will have every slow learner working—probably harder than he has ever worked before—and learning more, too. The experiments may be simple, or complex, but quantity is important. The children will get to associate science with doing experiments, which is one of your objectives. We are going to suggest a series of experiments. These are not unusual, nor difficult. You will be able to find the materials without too much trouble. But they are, as you will see, fun to do—and they do enable the children to make observations and to draw conclusions.

One other value of this method: it is intrinsic motivation—and can be used as a reward system if need be. You will find that the desire to do this type of work is great, even among the slowest learners, and you can use this to gain a large measure of self-control from this group.

Here are some experiments typical of the type you should use:

1. Optical illusions: "How is our sense of sight often fooled?"

    a) Draw three lines on three separate sheets of construction paper (Illustration 7-2), thus:

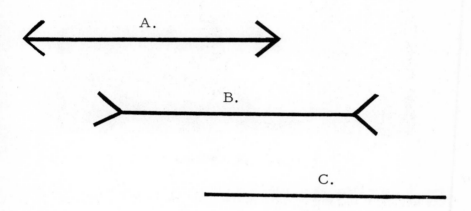

WHICH LINE IS LONGEST?
ARE THEY ALL EQUAL?

Illustration 7-2

Ask the children which line is longest. Have the children write their guesses on sheets of paper, and submit them. Calculate the results. You will probably find they are incorrect. Make sure you make the first line the longest. It appears just the opposite.

Remind the children they are submitting their observations, and you will inform them of the results of the group.

    b) This one is called "hole in the hand."

Roll up a piece of paper, or use a tube from a roll of paper toweling or even toilet tissue. Hold the tube with the *right hand,* placing it between the thumb and the forefinger, and

Illustration 7-3 (left)

holding it in front of the left eye. *Look through the left eye, keeping the right one open,* and voilà, the hole appears (Illustration 7-3).

c) Which card is largest?

Cut several cards in exactly this shape (Illustration 7-4):

Use various colored construction paper. Have the children hold the edges side by side, and record which they think is largest Then have them place them side by side, but reversed. Finally ask them to place one on top of another.

In each of these experiments, the eye is fooled. If you present them well, the children will do them over and over again, show them to friends and relatives, and really have fun—as well as learn.

2. If you have a friendly dentist, perhaps he will present you with a gift of some mercury. Allow your children to lift the bottle, to experience its weight. Then pour a bit into their palms, being sure they have removed any rings they are wearing. The material is unique because of its weight and because of the manner in

Illustration 7-3 (right)

which it forms small balls. You may allow the children to coat a penny to make it temporarily look like a dime. Your problem is "What is mercury, and what are some of its properties?"

3. When teaching static electricity, have the children mix some salt and pepper on a piece of paper. If they then run a comb through their hair quickly, and put the comb near the mixture, grains of one will jump to the comb—and the other will remain on the paper. Try this yourself to find out which is which. Incidentally, this will work only if the hair is relatively free from grease or hair spray. If you find it is not succeeding for every child, explain why.

These are relatively simple experiments, but they do foster understanding of scientific principles. Find appropriate ones to use, and don't hesitate to allow the children to try them. Both you and they will be enthused. To find suitable experiments, you have many resources:

1. Your curriculum bulletins and syllabi.
2. Textbooks—both those in current use, and those old copies

THE BANANA ILLUSION

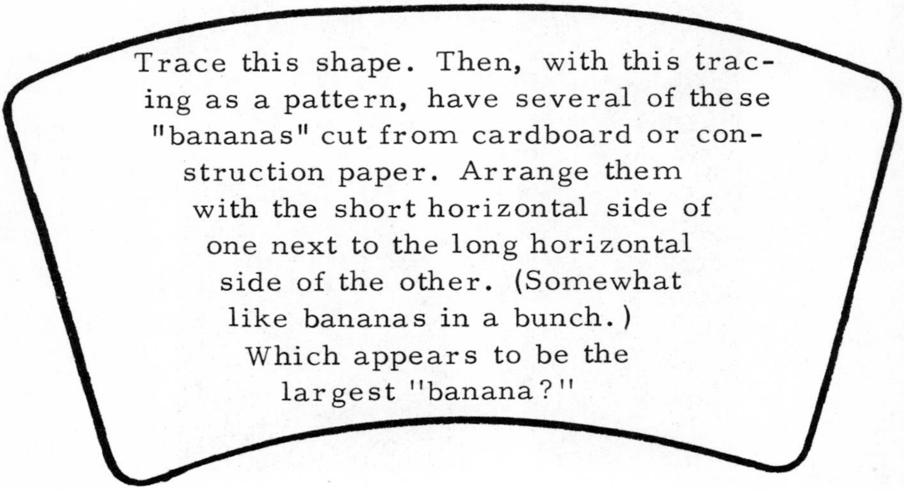

Trace this shape. Then, with this trac-
ing as a pattern, have several of these
"bananas" cut from cardboard or construction paper. Arrange them
with the short horizontal side of
one next to the long horizontal
side of the other. (Somewhat
like bananas in a bunch.)
Which appears to be the
largest "banana?"

Illustration 7-4

you may find in the school bookroom. We have found it
worthwhile to visit used book shops, too, for outdated science books, because these often contain excellent ideas.
Some of the best we have located came from texts over thirty
years old.

3. Your friends and other science teachers.
4. Your pupils. (The "hole in the hand" experiment was suggested to us by a child.)
5. Magazines—such as *Popular Mechanics*—often offer material
suitable for our purposes.
6. Workbooks and laboratory manuals.

We cannot emphasize this experimental approach too much. It
is the science teacher's main asset.

Demonstrations

Do demonstrations which will capture and hold the children's
interest.

There is, for example, a simple one in which the demonstrator turns water to wine, and "the wine" back to water again. The excitement this can generate is great, and the experiment can be done for class after class, because, while it is familiar to the teacher, the children haven't seen it. A colorless solution of phenolphthalein is prepared, which resembles water. Add it to a dilute base, and it turns a beautiful fuchsia color. Then add dilute acid, and presto, colorless again. Fun? Sure! Learning going on? Perhaps! Teaching going on? Of course! And so easy! Even if such experiments don't fit into the curriculum, they should be thrown in just to motivate the pupils.

Years ago there was a German scientist who was a real "character." He built a weather vane right through the roof of his house. He originated an experiment children love—pulling the "Magdeburg hemispheres" apart. Teams of horses couldn't do it—but boys love to try. Most science laboratories have the hemispheres; try them, but use a good pump, and seal the edges with Vaseline or water before you remove the air.

Try the chemical volcano. Ignite strips of magnesium, and insert the burning metal into a mound of ammonium dichromate. It's a wonderful device for motivation (Illustration 7-5).

Illustration 7-5

Another simple experiment, which is fascinating: Put some sugar into a beaker, and add concentrated sulfuric acid to it. You will produce carbon, but in a most unusual form.

Items of scientific interest

Encourage your children to bring into class items of scientific interest. Children will (if encouraged, and given credit for it) bring in such specimens as skulls (animal, to be sure), or plants (poison ivy, anyone?). The pièce de résistance which I received, however, was a deer fetus, five months old. The parent of a boy in one of my classes had accidentally killed a pregnant deer. (I subsequently discovered this is illegal.) We were presented with the baby deer, preserved in a large jar of formaldehyde. It was a perfectly beautiful creature, looking like all of the illustrations of Bambi you have ever seen. Children not in my classes would stop by my classroom, always with the same request: "Can I see your deer?"

Bulbs and plants, rocks and transistors, seeds of all kinds—the list of science items is endless. Nature should never cease to fascinate us—and it never will—if we do not permit our curiosity to die.

Taking children to visit a neighborhood pet shop is often worthwhile. They will be taught the proper way to handle animals, and enjoy the "merchandise" in the shop.

Pursue topics which capture your interest—or the children's

Try to follow their lead. If there is a topic in which they are interested, pursue it if you possibly can. My students loved rockets and space travel—perhaps because it intrigued me so much—so we studied it at great length. We also worked on the "Abominable Snowman" and on U.F.O.'s (Unidentified Flying Objects). Today you might consider the Loch Ness monster. (Is it really a dinosaur?) The cause of the big East Coast blackout in 1965; how to become rich prospecting for uranium; how to desalinate water; how to grow enough food to feed the entire world. You may wish to have the students tell about their findings. For the slow learner, oral reports are good and do not have to be too long. The children may show pictures, talk about radio or TV programs on the subject, or cite magazine or newspaper articles.

Always have interesting things on display in your classroom

One week I found a huge coffin in the corner—or so it appeared. Upon closer inspection, it turned out to be an iron lung, which a girl in the class had constructed: she purchased lumber from a lumber yard (which they had cut to size for her), she used a vacuum cleaner, and a homemade manometer. The most remarkable feature of this project was that, in an emergency, it could actually have functioned. Fortunately it served us only to decorate the room after it won First Prize at our science fair.

If you have science fairs, it is well worthwhile to exhibit the entries—whether they have won prizes or not. They represent the children's labors and encourage other youngsters to make attempts.

Fish tanks with tropical fish, a terrarium all add interest. To set up a terrarium, use any glass container which may be sealed. A fish tank with a glass plate on top is excellent. Place a mixture of soil and peat moss in the bottom, and plant some slow-growing plants in it. Water, cover, and seal, and place on a window sill with partial but not full sunshine (half day is best). You will find that if the terrarium is balanced, the plants will thrive. The water cycle is easily visible, for one can see the water collecting on the top and sides, and then running down into the soil.

Other plants, such as bulbs, are good because the children can see their progress as they grow and flower.

Science teachers are indeed fortunate, because the laboratory supply room is a veritable storehouse of surprises. Embryos of all kinds are on the shelves, waiting to be studied. Fossils (the ancient variety), models (the plaster variety), or unusual, preserved specimens can encourage the curiosity of even the slowest learner. Bring them into your classroom, and allow the children time to examine them. The time will be well spent. We are giving the children experiences, and these make a far more lasting impression than writing in their notebooks.

Microscopes, chemicals and dissections

Nothing makes a child feel as much like a scientist as looking into a microscope, mixing chemicals or doing a dissection of a lifeless specimen. In all of these areas your slow learner can be taught to excel, if you will give him diagrams, very specific oral instructions and encouragement. Actually, testing for the presence of an acid with litmus paper is far better than hearing your teacher describe it. Seeing the magnetic field, by sprinkling iron filings on a sheet of paper under which there is a magnet, is much more memorable than reading about it.

Laboratory specimens such as frogs (lifeless, of course) are available from biological supply houses at relatively small cost. Children will shy away from doing the dissection at first, but it does not take long before they are enjoying the work. If you give them a detailed diagram, they learn very quickly to identify the vital parts. You may have them dissect growing seeds, too. Using beans, you can force them to germinate by placing them between pieces of absorbent cotton on a dish, moistening and putting the dish in a warm place.

There are many simple chemical experiments, such as those suggested in toy chemistry sets. Be sure that any you permit the children to do are safe. You will find that only minute quantities of chemicals are necessary.

If you have microscopes available, try to give each child the experience of seeing a piece of moistened newspaper with printing. This will give him the concept of magnification beautifully for he sees the fibers in the paper and the ink. Other interesting specimens are a piece of human hair (particularly the root—but if you care to use this, be your own source), or cells scraped from the inside of your cheek and spread on a glass slide.

Collections and constructions

Encourage your children to collect rocks or leaves, seeds or flowers. Collecting can be exciting, and it surely supplies a feeling of achievement. By using a text, any child can identify his specimens. Since this is scientific work, emphasize care in making identifications. Give instructions to do the work neatly, and give credit for it toward the child's grade.

A rather novel twist would be to suggest collecting samples of fabrics, both natural and synthetic. Perhaps these might be studied under the microscope. Does cotton look different from fiberglass? Nylon from wool?

Many children enjoy constructing things. Crystal radios, walkie-talkies, simple motors, weather vanes, and wind socks may be constructed. If we can foster work of this nature, we may help a child discover talents he was never aware he possessed. Instructions are often available, as well as kits for these items. Our slow learners benefit greatly from this kind of work. Exhibit any worthwhile projects which are brought in.

The geological history on the area in which you live is often very interesting

You may reside on a hill caused by terminal moraine as we do, or near a lake produced by a glacier thousands of years ago. There are evidences of events which occurred millions of years ago, if we are able to read them. We may also wish to collect specimens of rocks which are found in our area. By a study of such geological phenomena, children become aware of their surroundings, and there are many interesting finds to be unearthed. Geology has played a tremendously important part in our history —consider the discovery of oil and of gold! We have no way of knowing what the future may bring, but we can prepare our children for it.

Astronomy and astrology

What two topics could be further apart?

Trips to a planetarium are in order—if one is available. Studying the moon and stars through a telescope is, of course, even more fascinating. By teaching the history of astronomy and of ancient peoples, we can bring out to our children how these unsophisticated people needed to feel their destinies were charted, and so adopted astrological beliefs.

It's fun to have the boys and girls bring in books on astrology, and show them how fortunes may apply to anyone. It is a rare person who does not consider himself to be kind or sensitive. If a person is told, "Be careful. The week of August 14 will be an eventful one for you," and some event does happen, which he may cause by his own nervousness, he says, "The stars were right." If nothing happens, he says, "Thank goodness I read in the stars about the impending danger and I warded it off." Lessons in astronomy are valuable to make of our children intelligent adults. Have the children bring in books, pamphlets or newspaper articles in regard to both and discuss them in class.

The space program—
America's future

NASA (National Aeronautics and Space Administration) will send a traveling show to your school. It has everything—from rockets to capsules to space stations. Your children will love it. They will love, too, a study of our astronauts, their jobs and their training; and of space stations, and our ultimate plans for settling on the moon. We are moving ahead at a tremendous pace—and, as a nation, we will need scientists in all fields to work for aerospace development.

Your slow learners will be enthralled by the study of space. Give them the opportunities to understand it—for example, the effects of weightlessness and escape velocity. Encourage the boys to build models of rockets, space stations and even space settlements. We have even taught young men to set off miniature rockets using carbon dioxide cartridges. Use a balloon, with the air rushing out of it and forcing it ahead, to explain rocket propulsion.

Years ago my girls wrote letters to try to find out why there are no women astronauts. We never did discover any reason! You may wish to bring up the topic for fun. The U.S.S.R. did have one.

Should you not discuss, along with the study of the exploration of space, the expenditure of the vast sums of money required? Would this money better be spent to eradicate poverty in all the areas of the earth?

Use slides to teach natural phenomena

It has been said that the badge of the tourist is the 35mm camera. Do you travel and take photographs? Have you ever thought of using your slides in your classes? They can be tied in with certain subjects in science, and through them the pupils can, at least partially, share some of your experiences. I now refer to Niagara Falls by the name bestowed upon it by one of my least impressed students, who declared, as I showed the most breathtaking pictures, "Hmmm—the Big Dripper." But, while he wasn't impressed, thirty other children were.

We take pictures of dams and hydroelectric plants, canyons and chasms, forests and petrified forests. They can be used to colorfully augment the curriculum.

Do not show so many, however, that the children get bored. Discuss with them just what they are looking at, so that the time is not wasted. Many of our children will never see the Natural Bridge of Virginia, or New Mexico's Carlsbad Caverns—unless we show them photographs.

Consumer education

Units in consumer education should be taught almost every year, to help our children understand how to buy intelligently—

and how to avoid being pressured by advertising. Have the youngsters observe the number of toys advertised on television from September until Christmas. Have them bring in examples of advertisements, and discuss them.

You may wish to introduce the children to *Consumer's Union,* and *Consumer's Reports,* or you may wish to have them read Upton Sinclair's book *The Jungle,* and newer books which inform the consumer of various practices and malpractices. Interpreting fraudulent advertising is important, and we can help our children to learn about it using magazines and newspapers.

Science for survival

There are many scientific truths which people need in order to avoid danger to themselves and their families. For example, "Never turn on an electrical appliance while standing in water" is a commandment which can literally be a life-saver. We suggest you cover all of the following:

1. Teach your children, "when you go out during a lightning storm, never stay under a tree."
2. Teach, "never put a penny into a fuse box, in place of a fuse. It transmits too much current, and is not safe."
3. Teach a knowledge of poisons and antidotes.
4. Teach how to put out various types of fires.
5. Teach how to stop bleeding, in case of an accident.
6. Teach how to aid a person choking on a piece of food.

Smoking

Every science class should spend some time on the topic of "smoking"—the possible effects it has on the lungs, and on the heart. Review statistics—you may easily obtain a great deal of material by telephoning your local chapter of the American Cancer Society or the American Heart Association.

Wherever possible, encourage the children to tell personal stories and anecdotes—and contribute stories of your own. Review the lesson on smoking in Chapter 2.

Narcotics

When children have reached the sixth grade, we must teach the topic of narcotics. For slow learners, we would suggest you invite members of the police force, or possibly show a film or film-strip as motivation for this unit. Because of the prevalence of narcotics, and the peddlers pushing them, we must forewarn our young people. Newspaper and magazine articles are excellent sources of information; we can use statistics to help tell the story, in this unit too.

It is important to teach some of the psychodynamics—to teach why some people need drugs and so readily become addicted. You will find your pupils anxious to discuss this problem, and very interested in it. Should there be stories in the local newspaper, be sure to use them. Bring the lessons as close to home as you can. If you have discussions, be sure the children realize the tremendous damage to themselves that drug addiction causes. This is one time you must have the last word.

Set up a class or school museum

Valuable projects may be contributed by students and teachers to establish a school "science museum." Working models are particularly fascinating, such as a van der Graf generator. Collections of any sort are worthwhile—leaves, flowers, and rocks are just a few—and you may wish to have the entire class work on each.

Unusual specimens may be created by your students. For example, two boys prepared a "Visible Chicken"—by boiling the chicken, lifeless, of course, removing all soft tissues, but retaining the bone structure. When a person saw this, there was no question about the relationship between reptiles (such as dinosaurs) and birds. It actually looked like a miniature dinosaur.

Sea shells, fossils, dioramas, charts, and pictures may also be made part of the museum. Slow learners can surely contribute to this. Be sure each specimen is well labeled. The work of each class will add to the interest, and the children will gain in status as they tell their parents, "My work is on exhibit in the school museum."

Fostering curiosity

To foster curiosity, you may wish to cite examples from Ripley's "Believe It or Not." Be sure, however, that any material used is fully explained. For example, the phenomenon of Siamese twins, which in earlier times might have been considered a man with two heads, must be discussed in terms of the embryological development. This condition is seen quite frequently in fish hatcheries, where such fish are called "sports." Mutations occur frequently—and children are interested in them.

Diet and exercise

In an era where we are more diet conscious, and more bikini conscious than ever before, wouldn't a unit of work on diet be valuable? If pupils have a knowledge of the caloric value of various foods, they can eat far more intelligently than otherwise. We suggest you teach this, though, in a meaningful way. Have the children list the foods they eat on any given day, and determine the caloric values. Then repeat this several times. This will be the basis for making up a personal "Calorie Book." When a child realizes a piece of pizza is about 400 calories, she may not eat it as often. A 500 calorie malted is not for the figure conscious.

Along with dieting, teach about our need for vitamins. The most graphic illustration may be that of a pregnant woman who doesn't get sufficient Vitamin B—her child may be born less intelligent than his cousin, whose mother was more vitamin conscious. For reducing diets, the vitamin and mineral supplement is absolutely essential.

Fad diets are dangerous, as is over-strenuous loss of weight. If your children have problems, and you wish to help them design reducing diets, encourage them to see their physicians first. By teaching this topic early in the boys' and girls' lives, you do much to prevent them from becoming very much overweight, which often has disastrous effects on the ego and self-image. Slow learners are easily able to grasp the concepts involved here— and can gain prestige in their families as a result of this kind of learning.

Exercises for developing
waistlines or biceps

You will discover many young people get relatively little exercise. Though they may be reluctant to admit it, they are very interested in their appearances. A unit on exercises which are appropriate to their needs is an excellent way to interest them. We suggest you initiate your work with the program outlined by the Royal Canadian Air Force. It is for all age groups, is within the ability of all youngsters and, as we can personally testify, it works extremely well. It is wise to obtain the physician's consent to this program.

As life becomes more sedentary (in front of the TV), and since less exercise is required in our daily work and in school, a program of this type can make a huge difference in the health of any boy or girl in your class.

You may wish to include some of the material from the President's Physical Fitness program as well, but these exercises are more difficult. Do not allow your children to feel defeated from the very beginning.

Children may start exercising as early as the first grade, and it is valuable to work some sort of calisthenics into the program each day. This may be connected with the Health Education program (Illustration 7-6). The teacher must thoroughly peruse the children's health record cards, to be sure that each child is permitted to partake in the exercises.

Biology moves ahead!

With the dawning of 1968 came the advent of heart transplants. Other major organs had been transplanted for many years—kid-

Illustration 7-6

neys, specifically since 1950. However, now physicians have been doing so with lungs and livers, as well as hearts. This is a subject which is fascinating from the legal and moral standpoint, as well as the medical aspect. Your slow learners will be impressed by your confidence in them if you discuss such topics, at their level of understanding, of course. You can cover the use of the scientific method—statement of the problem, hypothesizing of solutions, trying out the solutions, changing them where necessary, and finally solving the problem successfully—in terms of medical research.

Heart transplant operations are extremely dramatic, and covered well in the news media. Children may be encouraged to make scrapbooks, do follow-up studies on various cases, and become deeply involved in the subject. These activities are particularly good for the slow learner, for they encourage research, and much material is readily available.

Artificial hearts are a possibility within the near future. Discuss them, show diagrams, and make your children knowledgeable, for these are among the most important advances we may expect in years to come.

SUMMARY

The methods, techniques and strategies included in this chapter are designed to cajole the slow learner into becoming interested in science by giving him a variety of experiences in the classroom, and by encouraging him to relate his scientific learning to his past and present experiences outside the confines of the school. It is suggested that you have him do experiments very frequently, and that demonstrations are used very often when experiments are not feasible. A listing of sources of both experiments and demonstrations is included.

The sharing of children's experiences with their classmates is stimulated by encouraging them to bring in objects of scientific interest, and by pursuing academically, a study of topics which have caught the children's attention. By filling your classroom with objects with which the boys and girls are unfamiliar, by using scientific tools such as microscopes and bioscopes, by performing frequent experiments with chemicals, by doing dissections (but never on living material) you are constantly supplying them with experiences related to science. Encouraging children to collect lifeless specimens and learning about them through research help develop scientific curiosity.

Through introductions to particularly interesting topics such as evolution, geology, astronomy, and the space program, you can develop an interest in the slow learner, in areas that he may never have known existed.

There are certain learnings which are vital to the survival of the individual, and work on these is suggested; one such area is dealing with electricity. Another is the possible effects of smoking; and still another is narcotics. Diet and exercise, too, fall into this category. Lastly, it is suggested you discuss, explain and stimulate interest in one of the most exciting developments of all time—organ transplants.

We are certain you will be able to convey to your children

Illustration 7-7

the feelings of excitement and wonder which the successful teaching of science engenders (Illustration 7-7). Rather than slavishly following a curriculum, teach curiosity. Rather than paper and pencil tests, do chemical tests. You are in the enviable position of being able to bring to your slow learners the wonders of the universe, and you do this by making them wonder.

8

living lessons in arithmetic for slow learners

Arithmetic, and its older brother mathematics, need not be a dull or dismal subject for the slow learner. By ingenious teaching, you can make it entertaining. Basic in successfully teaching this subject to the slow learner is the use of diagnostic tests, followed by analysis of the results, to determine the child's needs. Then we suggest you teach the necessary material, and do drill work to reinforce the learning of the skills. Other suggestions you will find involve relating the study of this subject to the lives of the children so that there is practical value to their schooling. The price of guitars is far more interesting than the cost of chicken feed. Try to apply your examples to actual situations. Whenever you can, be sure to show the children the opportunities they have to use their knowledge of arithmetic in their own affairs.

A method for the preparation of diagnostic tests is included; there are techniques for drilling, which make it fun—contests, for example, and team games. The mathematics of daily living is discussed. It is suggested you use three-dimensional models whenever possible, to make geometry come to life. Consumer education is another unit included in this chapter, followed by budgeting allowances, puzzles, games. Discussions of inflation and deflation, the stock market, and the abacus are introduced. Special techniques dramatizing arithmetic, teaching the concept of zero, and using arithmetic fundamentals to decorate your classroom are given. Finally the utilization of unexpected quizzes is suggested.

DIAGNOSTIC TESTING

It is virtually impossible for any teacher to teach mathematics or arithmetic without being aware of the abilities of the youngsters in her class. To determine these, obtain or write some diagnostic tests. These need not be standardized, nor complex. A one-page mimeographed sheet can be all you need. Give ten examples in each of the basics, varying the problems in this manner: For addition:

3	5	132	$ 14.	$ 29.68
4	7	68	3.	4.02
7	16	7	100.	137.10
5	32	57	24.	9.16
1	9	369	18.	4.08
6	84	22	7.	34.19

5 feet 6 in.	14 feet 10 in.	3 quarts 1 pint
3 feet 4 in.	9 feet 8 in.	18 quarts

144 qts. 1 pint	12 lbs. 8 oz.
62 qts. 1 pint	8 lbs. 10 oz.

While each problem involves addition, other concepts are involved at the same time. Using work such as this, you can determine at what point a child needs help. With the slow learner, this is an absolute necessity. It makes no difference what grade a child is in—if he cannot add dollars and cents, he must be taught it.

Be honest with the children. Explain to them why you are giving them this test—that it is to help you to determine what their needs are. If a child is able to do the first three examples correctly, you may assume he can handle the addition of simple figures. If he makes errors in the fourth problem, give him additional diagnostic work in this—because he may have made care-less mistakes, and yet understand the concept. For the child who is careless, drilling will help, and the activities to be suggested will be of use. We suggest you include addition, subtraction, multiplication, division, decimals and fractions. (This is, of course, providing your children have advanced far enough to have been taught these. In the lower grades, include the material they should be able to handle.)

It seems obvious that no child can progress to more advanced concepts if he cannot handle fundamentals. Yet many times they are expected to do just this. There are cases where the teacher must either "throw out the curriculum," or if you are not per-mitted by your school system to do this, teach two curricula: the one for your grade, and the fundamental skills in which a child is lacking. We know of seventh grade children who, as we have said elsewhere in this book, cannot subtract. How can we ignore this, and teach other, more intricate, advanced material which, incidentally, that child may never need to use? Algebra is being taught to children who cannot handle fractions. Try to see this from the child's viewpoint, and you realize the quandary he is in. We believe you can do a great service for all of the children you teach, if you take this into consideration when you plan your lessons.

But, supposing you find a child who "blocks" when he tries to do an example containing fractions. If you have tried every de-vice you can think of, and nothing works, you will have to go on to something else; but try to return to these fractions later. You may find that the block has disappeared, and that, after some time has elapsed, the child is better able to learn.

Dare we call this a "common sense" approach? It is surely a logical way to handle the learning problems some of our children face in mathematics. We have also discovered that one teacher may succeed where another has failed. This does not necessarily mean that the first was a poor teacher. Each of us teaches dif-ferently; and one person's methods may be better with a partic-ular child than another's. Secondly, as children mature, they change, and these changes affect their ability to learn. Mary has been unable to comprehend decimals, and then, in the eighth grade Miss Smith has been able to teach them to her. Should all of the credit go to Miss Smith? The important thing is that now Mary is better able to handle this important area than she was previously. Should Miss Smith feel proud? Of course!

At the very beginning of the term, diagnose wherein your children's mathematical learning problems lie, and help them to solve them.

CONTESTS

Drill or a great deal of repetition is vitally necessary—particularly for children who learn slowly. How can we convert it into entertainment? One way is, of course, to convert the drills into contests. Here is a basic one, which you may vary to fit the needs of your children.

Make up a set of cards for each skill in which you wish to drill. You will need as many cards as there are children in your class. A card should contain approximately twenty-five examples—all of the same type. Give each set a letter, and then number the cards so that you will be able to identify them easily. Addition cards might be set A (Illustration 8-1). Subtraction set B, or set S, etc. Write five series of examples, or five rows of five examples each. A card would look like Illustration 8-1.

Instruct the children to add each example. Then they are to add the sums of the five examples in the top row, row A. Next they are to do the same for each row of five examples. When they submit their results to you, they will have a series of figures like this:

Row *a*)   64
Row *b*)   42
Row *c*)   110
Row *d*)   89
Row *e*)   69

These are easy to check, for you or your monitor. Instead of twenty-five numbers, you have five. The children have had five additional examples, when they have had to find the total of the sums for the examples in each row.

To use the cards, distribute them, and have each child tell you

A-15

a)					
6	3	42	584	1234	
18	23	68	625	567	
27	46	86	907	89	
34	59	99	654	1	
51	74	27	321	10	
				987	a) _____

b)					
$ .33	$ .39	$34.00	$502.60	$876.	
.51	1.29	4.29	88.50	543.	
.69	.88	6.48	9.42	210	
.74	.69	5.27	8.69	123	
.42	2.49	6.51	7.56	456	b) _____

c)					
$ .25	$420.	$904.	$870.	432.	
.49	56.	308.	886.	10.	
.08	780.	45.	88.	504.	
.06	65.	92.	686.	69.	
.85	498.	78.	703	783.	c) _____

d)					
$50.62	$12.08	$11.60	$276.55	$ .68	
65.49	14.06	3.59	65.05	.57	
27.25	18.09	22.68	842.35	.46	
86.50	25.05	18.68	98.49	.35	
86.50	49.03	6.60	270.86	.24	d) _____

e)					
32	496	871	636	761	
14	124	962	15	167	
59	532	103	3	77	
88	579	757	29	25	
76	61	59	178	20	
_____	_____	_____	_____	_____	e) _____

Illustration 8-1

which card he has. I, E, A4, B6. Record this, so that he will receive new cards each time you use the set.

Tell the children they are working for speed and accuracy. They must submit their results to you, and if they are correct they will be credited with this. To earn credit, they must do the entire card, in the time allotted. Keep a huge chart as a scorecard. On it list the name of every child in the class. When a child has completed a card correctly, place a flag, a star, a stripe, or any other form of indicator next to his name. Invest in several prizes, or have an Honor Roll in the front of the room, with the legend, "Our Medallion Mathematics Winners." At the end of every month, place the name of the boy and girl with the most cards correct, on this Honor Roll.

You will find that your boys and girls, to fulfill the requirements, will have to be careful, yet work rapidly. For the slow learners, prepare cards which are simpler than those of your other pupils. No one need be aware of this, since it is you who distribute the cards. You are able to individualize the work to fit the needs of the other children as well, by actually assigning cards to the boys and girls when you prepare your lesson.

By varying the skills, you are able to suit the drilling to the work needed. Is it multiplication? Construct a set of cards, and you have thirty or thirty-five different sets of problems for the children to work on. Use index cards, clearly labelled; they can be used and reused many times.

If there are some children who always win, give them handicaps in the form of cards with more examples, or set a time limit to do the twenty-five suggested. The hours you spend preparing the cards will prove an excellent investment. The class will be occupied, so that you will have an opportunity to work with the slow learners.

It is essential that the children get practice in skills, without becoming bored or resentful.

TEAM GAMES

Another way to disguise drilling is by having team games. First give a diagnostic test, to determine which children are strong in the subject, and which are weak. In setting up the teams, take this into account. You may wish to borrow a concept from the summer camping industry, and have "Olympic Games" and name each team for a participating nation. Assign a score-keeper to keep score on the board. Have the teams get on line, and call "batters up." Give the first two children a small problem. They are to work out the answers, and raise their hands as soon as they determine them. The first hand to be raised gives the answer aloud. If he is correct, he wins the point. If he is wrong, the other team gets the opportunity to answer. If this child is correct, they get the point.

After a child has responded, he moves to the back of the line. The first team to reach 50 points wins the game.

You may use any skill you wish, or combine many. Give your slow learners relatively simple problems at the beginning—making sure they are not frustrated immediately.

This kind of drilling is good because it adds an element of excitement to the class work. If you have a class newspaper, the headline for the lead article might be "Holland wins addition contest." Then, in the article, a list of the members of the winning team would appear. You might use three or even four teams, if you prefer.

In assigning the problems, use a rapid fire approach. Pitch the problems at the children. Keep a pressured atmosphere in the room. If the class needs review work on their fundamentals, you can use the Olympics as motivation. They will work more to perfect their skills for an activity such as this, than they will in later life when they *must* know how to add, or divide. To heighten the excitement, you may decorate the room with flags of the nations. Teams should be set up (and you must do this, so that they have some degree of equality), but you may allow them to choose their "country." Stress the team approach. Should you decide to do this, you can make it a term project, and post signs to show the progress of each team.

We are living in a time when young people "play it cool." Don't let them. You can get them stirred up, and excited by techniques such as this—and accomplish far more than if they are allowed to quietly do their work.

MATHEMATICS OF DAILY LIVING

If six cans of juice are on sale at 89 cents which normally cost 19 cents each, does it pay to buy six?

During the summer, a pair of boots is on sale at a 15 percent discount. Does it pay to buy them, rather than wait until the snow falls? The regular price is $22.

Your children should learn, from their mathematics and arithmetic classes, the practical, everyday aspects of the subject. In the lower grades, this involves handling money. You can make mock bills and coins, and should set up situations in which the children buy and sell items, so that they learn the value of quarters, dimes, and half-dollars. Include the fact that there are no wooden nickels and three dollar bills. From this a study of currency might develop.

In the upper grades, a study of taxes is valuable. Gasoline, cigarettes, and sales taxes are paid by all of us. Shouldn't our children understand them? Comprehending the income tax surely is important.

A knowledge of measurement is needed. You may have the children measure the blackboards and the pictures, the desks and the room. You may have the children determine each other's heights. The inch, the foot, the yard, the mile, and even the meter and kilometer are important to each child. Teach these by having the boys and girls do the actual measuring with string or paper, using rules and tape measures.

REALIA—USING REAL OBJECTS WHENEVER YOU CAN

Because the slow learners need concrete objects before they can master abstract concepts (Illustration 8-2), use as many real objects as possible, and choose these real objects from the children's personal experiences. If you are teaching the concept of three, show three books, three pencils, three crayons, three children. Have them draw three apples, and color them. Allow them

Illustration 8-2

to choose their own objects. In the upper grades, if you are teaching "sets" allow the boys and girls to choose their own objects for the set. When you discuss lengths, cut pieces of ribbon or construction paper into appropriate sizes. Show inches of wood, or ribbon, even of one's hair, of string. Do the same with centimeters. In discussing area or volume, have actual boxes to show specifically what it is you are talking about. You may take the children for a walk in the school yard, to measure it and determine the area.

Proceed from real objects to diagrams, and from the diagrams to abstractions. You may wish to use a felt board (literally a board covered with felt, to which paper adheres) to teach some of these concepts as well as fractions and decimals. Divide squares and rectangles as well as circles (Illustration 8-3). Have your children cut paper into parts representing the fractions or the decimals. Give them actual experiences (using special scissors prepared for child use), as well as visual ones to help build their comprehension.

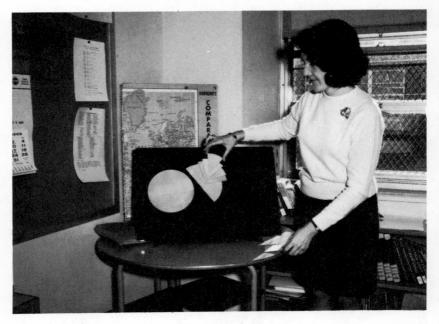

Illustration 8-3

GEOMETRY—LOOK AT THE MOON

Don't try to teach geometry without showing the children the specific geometric forms. Drawing them on the board is not enough; neither is pointing to the moon. Both are remote. If you are discussing a triangle, have one of your slow learners construct a large one of cardboard or construction paper. Do the same for rectangle or rhombus, circle or angle. Visualization is difficult, particularly for the slow learner; seeing the form simplifies working with it.

When the cube is taught, have a solid box available for reference. Cylinders, balls, shoe boxes—use any device but show exactly what you are talking about. In the beginning, isn't it far clearer to say "the area of *this* triangle is," and point to it than to say "the area of a triangle is ————," without showing the specific form. After doing this for a while, you will find the slow learner is able to visualize for himself.

Children can construct these figures, and your slow learners will be able to find shoe or gift boxes, measure them, and from these go on to more abstract thinking. Do not omit this activity because it seems too fundamental. Actually it may solve many problems for you, in helping your children make the transition from concrete to abstract thinking.

CONSUMER EDUCATION IN THE MATH CLASS

Children can and should be taught the basics of intelligent consumption. This can be done, for example, by asking them to compare the price of domestic canned meat, at 69 cents for 6 oz., with imported meat at $1.29 for a half pound.

Various brands of appliances may be much more expensive than those which are unadvertised. Have the children do research on this aspect of consumer education. Do detailed work on the discount stores. Are the prices lower? Have your children calculate discounts, on items which they are familiar. A phonograph record sells for $5.00, but it is sold at a 10 percent discount at another store. However, you must spend 40 cents carfare to get there. Does it pay to go to the shop giving the discount?

Even the simple device of "Sales" should be studied. Are items being sold "For Less" really bargains? Is 2 for 39 cents cheaper than 19 cents each? Why are items priced at $4.95 and $4.98, rather than $5.00?

Consumer education is particularly necessary for our slow learners. They will utilize it far more than discussions of "How many yards of fencing will Farmer Joe need to keep his pigs in their pen, if the pen is 120 feet by 160 feet?" Develop problems which will really help—making sure the children are aware of the money they can save—and you will find their interest will be stimulated.

SAVINGS BANKS—BETTER THAN
THE PIGGY BANK?

One four year old wanted to go to the savings bank alone.

"Why, dear?" his mother queried.

"They always give you the money, but if I go alone, maybe they'll give some to me."

Do your children understand savings banks? Have you ever wondered what they do with your money? You may decide to have the children do research work on this problem by visiting banks, and consulting with the management. Discuss the interest offered (about 5 percent) as opposed to the 7 percent which is charged to people borrowing money for mortgages.

Teach the difference between simple and compound interest. Are Christmas Club accounts more or less desirable than other savings accounts on which interest is paid?

If the children are affluent enough to open accounts, they might be encouraged to do so. Then have them compute the amount of money they are able to save if they deposit even very small sums regularly. It is interesting to discuss old accounts which have grown steadily because of the amount of interest that accumulated. Assume a dollar was deposited in the year 1800, for example. How much would the account have in it today?

GRAPHS

Have your children graph their own progress in mathematics. Even first or second graders can be taught to make simple graphs, and then can visualize their achievements. If you do this, make sure your slow learners are able to see improvement in their work. You can do this by testing them on their own level. As we have suggested, after you do diagnostic work with them, drill them, and then test them on this work. They should be able to achieve some success. If they do not understand a concept, reteach it. Try to help them to achieve an upward climb on their graphs.

Graphing such events as baseball scores, is interesting for the older child. You may also find some children interested in the Cost of Living Index, once you have explained it to them. Still others might work with the Dow Jones average—on a daily or weekly basis. The object of these graphs is to use statistics we find in the daily newspapers.

HOW DO YOU SPEND YOUR ALLOWANCE?

Budgeting money is so important, it should be taught in every mathematics or arithmetic class. You may teach it by having your children work out a budget for toys (in the very low grades). How much does a doll or train cost? What does her dress cost? Keep adding items, showing how expensive they are. Teach the children to determine whether or not they can afford to spend their money for these things. Older children can work out actual budgets for themselves. They may consider the boy or girl who has a job after school. You may have them work on budgets for families—considering couples with no children, with one or two, with eight; you may be interested in considering the budget of a family with a youngster in college.

The United States Printing Office offers material on this subject. Have your children write for their catalogue. Most of all, be sure you cover the specific meaning of "living within one's budget."

PUZZLES—FOR STIMULATING YOUR CHILDREN TO THINK

Puzzles help to make learning palatable. They mystify, and challenge, and make your class exciting. Try puzzles such as the following:

1. Tell the children to think of the age of any person they know. Using their own is too simple. Then they are to:
2. Multiply the first number by five. (If the age is 30, they would multiply the 3—that would be 15.)
3. Then add 3 (gives us 18).
4. Next double this figure. (Now we have 36.)
5. Then add the second number of his age, and give you the figure. (We still have 36.)
6. You subtract 6, and tell them the resulting number. (And we have our 30.)

After the children try this several times, and find that, if their arithmetic is correct it works, have them work out the reason why it is true.

Puzzles stimulate thought, are "conversation pieces," and enliven your class. Many collections have been compiled. You will find a number of them in the encyclopedias. They are a valuable added attraction to your class. Don't subtract the time they require because they will multiply your children's pleasure. Avoid an artificial division of work and play by the addition of such material. Your slow learners enjoy these activities, and they may very well surprise you with their abilities in these areas.

GAMES

Here are games skillful teachers have devised:

1. Speed: The teacher reads off a series of simple calculations in addition or subtraction, multiplication or division. Read them very quickly. The students who get them all correct win. For example, you might read:

   Two plus two, three plus nine, eight plus six, fourteen plus nine, six plus six.

   Or: Multiply 8×6, 5×9, 3×7, 2×4, 12×7.

   Use as many as ten combinations; when you initiate this game, go slowly. As the children adjust to it, quicken the pace. Your slow learners are encouraged to work more quickly. Very often there are the dawdlers, and this method pressures them to speed up.

2. Relationships: There are examples which are fun to do; try these with your children. They are to determine the relationships between the numbers. For instance:

   a. 1-2-4-7-11-16 what is the next number, and how did you determine it? (Here we added one to the first number, two to the second, three to the third, 22 would be next.)

   b. Another: 1-2-6-42, and the next?

   (This is a more difficult problem. We have added the square of the number to the number itself; one squared is one, two squared is four, etc. The next number is 1806.)

After calculating these relationships for a time, ask your children to develop some of them. You will be surprised.

INFLATION AND DEFLATION

How often we hear the words, "Prices are going up!" De we ever hear the opposite? Not within the writer's memory. How can we help our children to understand the concept of rising and falling prices, of the connection between supply and demand, the effects of a war on the economy, and the spiral of inflation ultimately causing deflation?

Both inflation and deflation affect us as individuals. We may find money growing either more or less valuable depending on the cycle at any given time.

You may wish to discuss the average salaried worker and how he is affected as his income changes. For example, he may earn more money and get higher wages, but this will buy less because prices have increased proportionally more than his income.

We believe that children are capable of understanding any topic, providing it is taught on their level of comprehension. Certainly, even fundamental knowledge of economics can prove to be extremely valuable. You can show how money changes in value from year to year, how prices change, and how the government, at times, attempts to control this.

For the slow learner, an introduction to economics at an early age may help him to master the subject much later on in his life, for early encounters help to make a subject far less formidable, and when it appears again, has the guise of an old friend. While all of the material may not have sunk in, some of it has.

THE BEARS AND THE BULLS

There is a popular singing group, appealing to the teen-agers, called "Dow Jones and the Industrials." We can see from this that the stock market has definitely "made the scene." Many, many people have gone through their entire lives not understanding very much about stocks, the stock market, and the bears and the bulls. There are many aspects of this subject which you may easily tie in to the mathematics program. The rise and fall in price of stock, the dividends paid, the number of shares sold by a corporation in terms of the assets the company holds, all are interesting. You can have your students set up a mythical company, issue stock (common and preferred), calculate the price rise or decline in the value of the stock as you set up varying conditions. Your company might have a board of directors; you could have meetings of all the stockholders, and even have a tycoon try to buy up the company. Or you might take the class to visit a stock brokerage, to see the ticker tape in action. If you are near New York or Chicago, a visit to the Stock Exchange is easily arranged. You can explain to your children how the business world, particularly the stock market, is affected by world conditions.

Don't fail to bring in the Federal Securities Act of 1933, and the Securities Exchange Act of 1934. Show how stocks may be sold for more than they are worth.

Your slow learners can absorb concepts about stocks—but be sure to teach this material at their level.

THE ABACUS

Pronounced ab' ah kus, the abacus was used by the ancients, the Greeks and the Romans, although we associate it with the Chinese. It's one of the forerunners of the digital computer, and it's possible for children to construct one themselves. The value of the device lies in the fact that it makes it possible for a child to visualize place values, and it was used at one time to teach addition and subtraction. You may wish to use it for that purpose. The children can actually handle it themselves; consequently it is of particular value in teaching the slow learner.

In constructing an abacus, decide first how large to make it, remembering that it can function even with two or three vertical wires. The beads on the wire to the extreme right are used to represent the numbers from one through nine. Above the horizontal crossbar, each bead is worth five units; those below the bar are worth one. The next wire holds beads representing tens. The two above the crossbar are worth fifty, those below ten.

You may use this device for slow learners, because they actually move the beads when they "take away," away from the horizontal bar, and when they add by moving the beads toward it. The construction of an abacus requires understanding, and it is worth having the children construct their own. This kind of personal experience helps many children when other methods fail. It is also a good source of physical activity.

UNEXPECTED QUIZZES

If you find you cannot encourage your children to study, you may wish to give unexpected, short examinations. We have found that these will keep older children "on their toes." It may be necessary to give your slow learners different material from that which you are presenting to the rest of the group. Fit the quiz to the needs of the child. However, we have found that these will get far more attention than a large, weekly or monthly test. Where a child is not making sufficient progress, this will be easily visible if you request the parent to sign the paper, and in this way you make both parent and child aware of the need for more intensive work. Make sure you accompany these quizzes with explanations. The work must be reviewed thoroughly, so that the children know exactly what is expected of them.

DRAMATIZATION

For slow learners, whenever you are able to present a subject dramatically, we suggest that you do so. For very young children, you may wish to try some of the following devices:

a) For teaching addition, a playlet using a rhyme such as this may help:

One little boy went to the zoo.
His sister went along, and then there were two.
Two little people off on a spree,
A friend went along, and now there were three.
Three young people went out the door.
They were joined by their brother, now there were four.

> Four youngsters, glad to be alive,
> Were joined by another, and now there were five.

As the first line is recited by a boy, he acts out the part. Then he is joined by a girl, and so on. The children see the people, and hear the number associated. They add the one person at a time, as he or she is added in the activity.

b) For subtraction, try this verse:

Teach the words of this little poem to the children. Then, as they sing, or speak the words, you point to the children who will carry out the action.

> Five little rabbits, sitting near the door.
> One ran away, and now there are four.
> Four little rabbits playing with me.
> One ran home and now there are three.
> Three little rabbits looking at you,
> One hopped away, and now there are two.
> Two little rabbits basking in the sun.
> Jimmy took one, and now there's just one.
> One little rabbit left all alone,
> He's gone home to have his dinner, and so there are none.

This dramatic approach makes arithmetic fun for the young children, and provides physical activity which is an absolute necessity for health. You will find games such as this will refresh them. The slow learner is helped with his arithmetic because he is dealing with concrete examples, from which he may be able to change over to abstractions.

Children love to compose jingles such as this one. Suggest this to them, and see what they bring into class.

TEACHING THE CONCEPT OF ZERO

Many teachers experience difficulty teaching the concept of zero, and particularly multiplication by the zero. We suggest you use this method:

Ask the children how many rows of desks there are in the classroom. (*Call on your slow learner for this.*) Write the number of desks on the board. Designate each row of desks with a number (Row 1, 2, etc.).

How many children are there in row 1? (*About 6.*)

Have the children sitting in the first row come to the front of the room.

How many children are there now in the first row?

Get from the children there are no children sitting in row 1 (1×0 equals zero).

Next have the children from row 2 go to the front of the room. How many children remain in rows 1 and 2? Zero. By gesturing, show that 2×0 equals 0. Do this until you have moved all of the children to the front of the room, and no matter how large a number you multiply by zero, the result is still zero.

This device entices the attention of the young children, and again is a concrete, rather than an abstract example of a fact in arithmetic.

CHILDREN'S CONTRIBUTIONS

An interesting assignment, on any grade level, is to have the children prepare problems for their classmates to solve. Choose one child, and have him present his problem. The first child to solve it correctly presents his. Encourage the children to try to "stump their classmates," but the problems must be solvable. Also suggest they introduce some humor.

USING ARITHMETIC TO DECORATE YOUR ROOM

When you are working with a particular topic, you may give the children an assignment to make designs relative to the topic being studied. In the lower grades, when teaching numbers, they may draw four—four apples, toys, people, or Santa Clauses, etc. At Easter, three bunnies, three eggs, etc. In the upper grades, geometric figures, for example, may be used to decorate. Graphs, problems of area, of discounts, of installment buying or finance companies, all of these may be diagramed, and used to attract the children's interest—by being posted in your room.

SUMMARY

Mathematics is the most logical of all of the subjects we teach, and it consequently should be taught in a logical manner. Just as a building cannot be constructed starting with the fifth floor, a child cannot be taught mathematics without knowing the fundamental arithmetical skills. Therefore, it is essential that you do diagnostic work with each slow learner entering your class to determine at which point he had stopped learning. Starting at that point, you can try to teach him the skills he needs, and then continue with new work appropriate to his grade and level.

Techniques are suggested for both diagnosis and for drilling. The latter are in the form of games, which are a very palatable way to present these very much needed activities.

We feel that all school work should be related to the children's lives, whenever possible, and we have included a section on the mathematics of daily living. For slow learners, this is essential since every child must be taught, for example, to handle money. Because slow learners often may experience difficulty handling abstractions, we suggest you use real objects whenever possible. (An empty frozen juice can is a perfect cylinder.) Circles, triangles, and cubes are far more easily understood if they are seen and handled first.

To broaden the children's field of knowledge, we have included units on related areas—consumer education, the stock market, and inflation and deflation.

Budgeting one's money, having the children graph their own progress, puzzles, and math games are suggested. For the young children, there are dramatizations for teaching addition and subtraction, and for teaching the concept of zero. Ideas for decorating your room with material related to math concepts are given. The strategy is suggested, too, that you may wish to give frequent, unexpected quizzes rather than formal, long examinations.

Basic to all of this is the idea of relating the teaching to the slow learner's needs, to his interests, and to stimulating him to think and to be interested in, rather than afraid of, arithmetic or mathematics.

9

dealing effectively with
parents
of slow learners

What more important ally might a teacher have in dealing with the slow learner than the people who are closest to him—namely his parents? If we approach the mother and father with genuine interest and sensitivity, we can undoubtedly obtain their cooperation throughout the child's school life. Frequent conferences with the parents of the slow learner are almost mandatory; for very often, the slow learner seems to be the forgotten child. We must be careful, too, not to appear defensive or hostile.

The concept for us to present to the parent is always, "What can we do, working together, to help your child?" It is important that we have a working knowledge of the child and of his home environment, and that we are aware of any problems which confront him in either his home or school life. By making the parents cognizant of the work being done in school, and of our efforts on behalf of their child, we can win their confidence and help, and hopefully promote improvement in the child's work. Hostility toward the parent, regardless of provocation, must be rigidly avoided. Suggestions, constructive comments, appreciation of whatever efforts the parents have been making to promote the child's learning, and voicing warmth and enthusiasm that is genuinely felt by the teacher will do much toward gaining the help we need from the parents. Remembering that the parents' influence on the child can either help or hinder our work, we must show them we are sincere and deserve their good will and cooperation. If at home they voice sentiments of derogatory nature concerning the teacher or the school, our work is set back and the child's learning impeded. On the other hand, if the parents have faith in us, in our methods and in our sincere intentions of helping the child to the best of our ability, they will willingly work with us, and the slow learner has a far better chance of improving his school work.

In this chapter we include techniques and strategies that you may use in speaking to the parents, based on the philosophy we have outlined. We suggest you show them how and why you use the methods you do, and the resulting progress the child has made. We constantly and consistently stress the positive approach —always encouraging both the parents and the child in their efforts to achieve learning. Because so many parents have requested it of us, and because we feel it has value, we have included a detailed series of instructions and suggestions on "How to Study," which you may wish to mimeograph and distribute to your children. Far too often, throughout a child's school career, no teacher stops to teach these study skills, which are so extremely necessary, particularly to the slow learner.

Throughout the chapter, we emphasize the positive approach. "What can *we* do," you ask the parent, "working together, to help your child?" The slow learner desperately needs both of us, working together to help him, if he is to improve.

ENLISTING THE AID OF THE PARENT

The headlines scream—"Parents Fight for Control of the Schools!" "Parents Seek to Dictate School Policy!" Long silent, parents now are asking for more influence in running the schools. One factor is overlooked completely—the work of the teacher and the *individual* parent to help the *individual* child. To use the jargon of the day, such "dialogue" is extremely necessary; not perhaps for every child, and every parent, but certainly for the slow learner. Consequently, let us discuss your relationship with a parent of one of these children. It is the parent whom we call your "essential ally."

Not all parents are satisfied with the education their children are getting; not all parents are "on our side." Certainly there are areas of our nation where it seems much of the blame for all social, economic and other ills is placed at our feet. There are hostile, unpleasant parents—some with justification, but surely not all. However, in dealing with any of them, hostile or not, there is one overriding factor which we will stress again and again.

When you tell a parent, "We are both working to help your child. We must work together with this goal in mind, and we cannot undermine each other, because, if we do, it is the child who loses"—you are using the most powerful weapon you have—your integrity, your profession. We are assuming that what you are saying is true. If you are not interested in helping the slow learner, your argument will not stand up, but if you can go on to say, "I have tried this" and then give the details, and the result, you will find even the most resistant will listen to you. If you then continue, "That wasn't too successful, so the next thing I thought of was—," are you not giving a most convincing argument? If you have honestly tried to work with the child, the parent's hostility will, 99 times out of the proverbial 100, disappear. There is nothing so convincing as the truth.

For example, Mrs. Jones comes to you saying, "Why is Mary Beth so far behind in her reading?" It is not fair to ask this question of you, because it reflects problems which have been developing since early in the child's school life. Nevertheless, if you are able to report, "Let me show you, Mrs. Jones, what we have been doing. There are many skills involved in reading. We have been working on a number of them. We have just studied picking out the main idea in a paragraph. Mary Beth still has trouble, but she can now recognize this with a certain amount of accuracy. We are also reviewing vocabulary words; for example, we discussed the prefix 'trans' and the words we find containing it—transport, transatlantic, transcontinental, transmit—this sort of thing. We have covered a number of prefixes. This is one method we use to build up a child's knowledge of words."—you are actually showing what you are doing to help Mary Beth. This is what Mrs. Jones is concerned with, and this should be her concern (Illustration 9-1).

As you speak to this parent, or to any parent, you must do a number of things:

Illustration 9-1

Take pride in the child's accomplishments

You must genuinely feel an interest in the child's intellectual and spiritual welfare. If you really feel this, the parent will sense it, and his feeling toward you will not be one of animosity, but of warmth and cooperation. This can be demonstrated by saying to the parent, "Mary Jane has improved in her work on fractions; she is now able to add and subtract them without difficulty." Then substantiate your statement by showing her the child's written work.

If you do not feel a definite interest in the development of the child, the parent is sure to sense your indifference, and nothing but hostility will arise. You will gain far less than nothing! Ascertain the specific problem causing the parent's hostility and, if you can, help her as well as her child. Take the attitude a fine doctor takes toward his patients. If a patient is irascible, the dedicated doctor probes for the cause of the trouble. Remember—a teacher is a nurse, a doctor, a priest, a psychologist, and above all, a true friend.

Gain the cooperation of the parent

Even if the parent is hostile, you must not allow yourself to react with hostility toward him. You are, after all, doing the best job you can, and are not threatened, psychologically, by this parent. Your task is to gain his cooperation, and you do this, as we have said, by showing what you have done and are doing to help his child, and suggesting ways that he may be of assistance.

Is the child remiss about handing in his homework? Ask the parent if he would be willing to check on the assignments to see if they have been done, and sign them. This indicates his interest in the child. Children do want their parents to be interested— they may behave as if this were a great inconvenience, but it is a concrete manifestation of parental concern, and, basically children crave this.

Does the child squint? Ask the parent to check with an eye doctor, to be sure glasses are not needed. Some children's eyes change during the intermediate years, and it is quite possible that glasses would be prescribed.

Is the child careless about his personal habits? Surely a parent should be informed of this—in a tactful way, of course. "Sometimes Joseph comes into school looking as neat and clean as possible. But there are other times when he forgets to wash his hands or comb his hair. Would it be possible for you to remind him before he leaves the house in the morning?" Underlying it all— *What can we do, working together, to help this child?*

Educate the parent

Explain specifically what you are doing, so that he understands your methods and your motivation. Show him that you understand the manifold problems that beset parents today— that the work of the parent is not an easy one and that, working together, the child can be helped. Hold frequent conferences with the parent reflecting a genuine interest on your part in the progress the child is making.

If you are asked to explain a grade, do not go on the defensive

Many times, pupils paint a completely false picture for their parents—and it lasts until the report card reaches home. "I can't understand it," John said. "I was doing 70 percent work, and he gave me a 55." So the parent goes up to see the teacher, annoyed at the injustice, and feeling this is a decided nuisance. You are the teacher. If you are using a system such as the one we outlined earlier, you have but to refer to your record book. "John," you say, "did well in the first test, but then he started downhill. He failed to hand in two homework assignments, one of which was a report involving a good deal of research. He received a 50 percent in another test, and a 60 in a third. I can see why he thought he deserved a 70. He was judging from the results of that first test. Many children will do just this. They will try to coast. I think that we had better discuss this with him. If you would care to make sure that he completes his work, that would help, I am sure. It probably won't be necessary indefinitely, but it would help for the time being, until we can rebuild his habits."

BE CONSTRUCTIVE

When you speak to parents, offer suggestions. Set out to win the parent's confidence. We have found that most of them do exhibit a feeling of respect and will consider what you have to say very carefully, in spite of what their children may tell them about you. One second grade teacher had a sign printed which she exhibited when parents were coming to visit. It read, "If you don't believe what they tell you about me, I won't believe what they tell me about you." And tell they do! This is why, when you meet parents, you must not antagonize them. A child may say, "Miss X hates me. She never even smiles at me." When the parent meets

Miss X, he finds she has a tendency to be a serious teacher, not prone to smile easily. What further impression does he get of her? Is she just mean, or is she involved in her work, and so intent upon it that she is tense, unsmiling. The parent may leave thinking, "Alice is right. She is mean." Or he may depart with the idea, "What a hard-working young woman. Alice just doesn't understand her. I must explain it." The impression you create can help or hinder you greatly. We are not out to win popularity contests, but we must attempt to give the impression that we are dedicated professionals, which most of us are. If you conduct yourself in an interested, professional manner, using the positive approach— again, "What can we do to help your child?"—the results are well worth your time and effort.

If, on the other hand, you announce, as we have heard teachers say, "You're Mrs. Johnson? Billy's mother? Your son is a pest. He's cute, but he is such a nuisance! He jumps up and down, and runs around the room, and he reminds me of a monkey who got out of his cage. What do you feed him—peanuts?" How would you feel if you were Mrs. Johnson? What would your reaction be?

Let us assume that every word you said is true. Could it not be said in another way? "How do you do, Mrs. Johnson. I'm sorry I had to disturb you by requesting you come in to school, but I felt I had to talk to you about William. I know you are interested in his education." Here you would pause, so that she could affirm this. And, of course, she is. Then you would continue, "I'm afraid he is going to fall behind in his work, because he doesn't give it his undivided attention. He has a great deal of energy, doesn't he? I know if we can influence him to use it constructively, to help himself, he will accomplish much more than he is doing now. What do you think? Has he told you about our English class?"

Of course he hasn't—what child would? So you go on to say, very gingerly, "He does begin the assignment, but he doesn't work at it until he finishes it. We have to work on that with him. Or he will get out of his seat, and waste his time throwing papers into the waste basket, instead of reading what has been assigned. We're anxious to get him over on to the right path. Can you help me?"

This positive approach can't miss. You can get every idea across, yet smooth the parent's ruffled feathers. We have been forced to suspend children, yet have the parents say to us, "Thank you for all you have tried to do for my child." Every mother or father wants to feel he or she is helping the child, doing the best he can for him. You are appealing to this instinct. How can you help but succeed?

If you are teaching pupils who have problems (The first guidance counselor we worked with stated it so well, "There are no problem children, only children with problems.") you must be concerned with how to help them. A disruptive child is a problem to you, but to the parent you would never admit that. It is always, "Bob could do so well, if he tried. He seems to be reluctant to work along with us. Do you think you might talk to him? He is missing out on so much."

John shouts out, usually obscenities, which he may have learned in his own home. Never, never refer to this. It is always, "John hasn't learned to curb his enthusiasm or his words. If he's going to do well in school he must learn this. Can you discuss it with him?" You must approach any visitor calmly, speaking in an educated, professional manner, with the vocabulary of an intelligent person.

PARENT VISITATION PROGRAMS

If this program is scheduled early in the school year, it is not as valuable as it might be later. However, it is still important that you encourage your pupils to invite their parents. Motivate them by discussing the visits for days before. Have pupils' work attractively displayed all around the room. Plan your lessons so that they reflect the work the classes have been doing. Whenever possible, plan for a lesson involving the maximum amount of pupil participation, always being mindful of the needs and intellectual limitations of the slow learners. For example, in languages arts or social studies classes, you might have a debate scheduled for one day—and parents might be specially invited to hear it. In science, laboratory work is of interest, particularly to a parent whose background probably did not include dissecting a fetal pig. You might decide to allow the slow learner to actually perform the dissection—with the assistance of the other children.

Always show your willingness to speak with parents. If during Open School Week, there is a special time set aside for parent-teacher conferences, have a sign to that effect displayed prominently in your room. If, during your class, you are too busy, smile pleasantly and say, "Can't we make an appointment? I would be very happy to speak to you at another time."

During teacher-parent conferences, at this time or any other, use the positive approach we have outlined. There is always some charming comment you are able to make—even if it is a superficial one, such as, "Lisa is such a lovely child. I know she's quiet. (She barely speaks, but you don't say that.) We hope to draw her out before the term is over. How does she behave at home?" From that question you may learn how to draw Lisa out—or, at the least, gain some insight into her behavior. For the disadvantaged child, why not say to the parent, whenever you get the opportunity, "Harold always looks so well groomed. I'm sure you must work very hard . . . ?"

Teachers often say, "It's a pleasure to have John in my class. He's always interested in the lesson." Why? Why say something nice? To do many things—to make the parent comfortable, to allay his feelings of anxiety which most people carry with them when they come into school, to gain his confidence, and most important, to enlist his cooperation on the child's behalf, to influence him to help his child, and in the process, to help you, the teacher.

LEARNING TO COMMUNICATE

You may have to telephone the parents of slow learners or send for them. Even then, in fact more important then, present anything favorable you can say first. "Richard passed a science test yesterday. I'm delighted. I knew he could do it. I asked you to come in before this happened, because I felt he wasn't paying enough attention to his work. But now he proved himself. I know you'll stress this to him. He can do it!"

This phrase, "He can do it!" is invaluable. It holds up hope, confidence in this child. If he believes it, if his parents believe it, he will try. Then it is up to you, the teacher, to help him.

"Jane did her assignment last night. I must show it to you

because it is excellent. It is the first assignment she has handed in—but you can see it shows she can do it! I know you realize how important education is. We want Jane to have the best. I'm sure you do, too." How much better this is than saying, "Your daughter is lazy. She's so interested in boys she has no time to do her homework. She finally handed in one assignment. Congratulations! It's about time."

Exaggerated? Surely. But teachers do get adverse feelings across to parents—far too often. <u>Never, ever be sarcastic.</u> You must get your constructive comments across with all of the enthusiasm you can muster. If you feel a child has a serious problem, refer the parents to the guidance counselor—but always tell them first what specific steps you have taken, what you have personally done to help their child.

There are times when you see many parents for relatively short periods of time—three to five minutes. To make even this bit valuable, try to be specific. You may say, "I believe your child is doing quite nicely. He is particularly strong in—(fractions, compositions, laboratory work, debating)." By saying this, you show you know the child. It might be necessary for you to say, "He is particularly weak in spelling, or multiplication," but again, be specific. If you can truthfully say to a parent, "I enjoy having your son in my class. He's so interested in science," say so, by all means. Handle any weaknesses the child may have deftly, being careful not to antagonize the parent, for as we have said, you need his help. Antagonism accomplishes nothing but animosity. This is one of the gravest problems in the world today, as anyone knows who reads the newspapers.

In speaking to parents, you may want to ask, "Are there any problems with Sue Ellen at home?" Or, "Does Sammy wear glasses? I've noticed him squinting." Any interest you show in the child usually is appreciated. Before the parent leaves, you may want to ask, "Is there anything I can do to help you?" Often there may be a problem, financial or emotional, which you may help to solve. For example, if a parent is unable to work, or is ill, you may work with the guidance counselor to obtain welfare assistance. If there is illness, the school nurse may be able to assist by telling the parent where competent medical aid may be secured.

By showing a genuine interest in the child's family, you may unearth problems that will help you to understand the difficulties which confront the child in his family environment. A sick father; a mentally ill mother; poverty, financial or cultural, are but a few of the many disasters our children face.

Too often, conferences are held before we get a chance to really learn to know a child. Then the teacher may say, "I haven't yet learned enough about your son, Mrs. Smith. Please sit down and tell me all about him." Use your seating plan and your record book to identify the child you are discussing.

There is one remark which makes a teacher very unpopular with the school administrators. Please—never, but *never* say, "Your child is too bright. He doesn't belong in this class." If you have this complaint, please see someone in the guidance department or a supervisor but don't tell it to the parents! It is wrong to do so, for many reasons. Sometimes a child is in a specific class because of his reading level, because of his previous grades, because of his abilities or disabilities in various subjects. For instance, he may be an excellent student in arithmetic, but poor in language arts. If you are interested, speak to the grade advisor, the guidance counselor, an assistant principal, or even the principal, but do not tell it to the parents.

Many parents will tell you, "My child doesn't know how to study." If it is true—let us stress the development of good study habits. You may want to use the following material in part or whole, or to make variations; but you will find it a most valuable lesson, and one which you may refer to in each parent conference. We have found it worthwhile to duplicate it, distribute it to our children, have them take it home to be signed by the parents, and then placed in the children's notebooks. Remember—it's not the only way to study, but it does give boys and girls some helpful ideas, and even more important, a place to begin. Discuss it with them, and make sure they understand how they may apply these ideas to their own lives.

HOW TO STUDY

What do we mean by studying?
We might say many things—understanding, memorizing, prob-

lem solving, but, above all, mastering material—making it a part of our body of knowledge.

How shall I study? These rules are not new, but they have helped many people. Try them, and see if any of them help you.

1. If you do your studying only to please your teacher, or do well on tests, you cheat yourself. You will get out of this only what you put into it. If you give it your attention, you will find the material will "stick," but if you daydream or become diverted, your time will not be productive.
2. Try to interest yourself in your assignments. Find things in them which are of interest to you.
3. Set aside a definite time and place to study. Don't leave your work until late in the evening, when you are tired. Immediately after dinner is far better.
4. If you can find a quiet place, use it. If not, it may be necessary for you to use the public library, or an area in your school reserved for this. Noise, music, radio and television are all distractions which you must avoid. You cannot study well with music blaring. If you think you can, you're fooling yourself.
5. Have everything you need available—textbooks, notebooks, papers, pens, pencils. Do not jump up and down.
6. Start to work immediately. It has been said by one famous failure, "Work fascinates me. I could look at it for hours." Don't. Begin as soon as you sit down.
7. Determine specifically what you must do to complete an assignment. If you are told to study it, to learn it, or that you are getting a test in it, use the following method:
   a. Read the material for which you are responsible. (This may be in your notebook or in a textbook.)
   b. Make an outline of the major topics.
   c. Fill in the details.
   d. Put your outline aside, and write another list, this time seeing whether you remember all of the major and minor items.
   e. If not, refer back to the source again.
   f. Do this until you know all of the material, and can do a full outline without looking at your source.

This method is good because you are learning concepts or facts in relation to one another. No one item is isolated. It has been found that related material is far easier to learn.

8. Another method, slightly different, is useful; particularly when you are working with a chapter in a textbook:

    a. Convert each chapter into a series of questions. As you read them list the questions.

    b. After reading the chapter, close the book, and answer the questions.

    c. For any questions you cannot answer, consult the text.

    d. Reread any material you need to learn.

    e. Your work is completed when you are able to answer each chapter question from memory; and the answer is correct, according to the text.

9. Think about what you are doing, and be sure you understand each topic thoroughly. If you do not, study it after you look it up. Merely finding the answer is not enough. Learn it!

10. Learn all the work assigned to you each day. If you will reread your notes, or your text, spending about twenty minutes to one half hour on each subject, you will find you need far less time before you take a test.

11. If you are absent, make up any work you miss as quickly as possible.

12. A word a day: If you are willing to learn one new word each day, your vocabulary will grow as if by magic. You may use your dictionary for this. Make a list of five words each week—new ones—and learn them. You will find a great deal of satisfaction in this each time you meet a word you have purposely learned.

13. If you find you need help, get it as soon as you can. Don't ever allow yourself to fall behind.

14. Each person must find a way to fix material in his brain. Some people do well by writing it again and again, others by reading it aloud. Still others by reading it silently, over and over. Probably the best way is to teach it to another person, or discuss it thoroughly with someone who is truly interested.

However you study, remember—you cannot learn if you are not actively thinking of what you are doing. It is almost impossible if you have the phonograph or television or radio blasting, if other people are speaking, or if you are uncomfortable or hungry. To learn, you must give your work your absolutely undivided attention.

Nor can you learn if you are tired. One hour of work in the morning is worth three at night.

15. Before any test, particularly important ones, follow these rules:
    a. Get enough sleep. You can't even read well if you are sleepy.
    b. Have any equipment ready the night before.
    c. Eat a good breakfast. You must have blood sugar for energy.
    d. Read the questions carefully. Many students lose credit because they are careless. Answer the question—not what you read into it, but what it actually calls for.

SUMMARY

The importance of gaining the cooperation of the parent, particularly of the slow learner, cannot be overestimated. If the parent is hostile, his child will often be hostile, as a result of the attitudes he has learned at home. If the parent is cooperative, he can help you to reach his child, and to improve his learning.

We have discussed several ways in which you are able to enlist the parent's aid. They are all based on the psychological point of view. "How best can we, working together, parent and teacher, help your child?"

You must feel a genuine interest in children. You cannot react with hostility, even to a hostile parent. You must, when necessary, educate the parent. You should never become defensive, but must offer constructive suggestions. By encouraging children, and their parents, you help to build the child's self-image.

Let us be particularly zealous in winning the cooperation of the parents of our slow learners for they, far more than the other children, need the help and understanding that we must endeavor to obtain for them.

10

using classrooms
"away from school":
group trips for slow learners

One of the features often characterizing the slow learner is his lack of cultural background. He has rarely been introduced to any sort of cultural experiences by his parents, or by his teachers. For example, let us consider traveling as one of these. This year a record number of Americans will go abroad. Within our country, too, it seems the nation is truly "on wheels." People are going more places, doing more things than ever before. But not everyone; a huge segment of our population never leaves home. Most often the reason is financial. But there are others: Inertia, or just plain laziness for one; lack of interest for another; illness or unawareness for a third. Almost always you will find your slow learner among the stay-at-homes—not because he wants to, but because he has to. Why shouldn't school try to break this pattern, by showing the child that there are fascinating places to be found, frequently and literally within a stone's throw of home?

We suggest you utilize group trips as one of your most important teaching tools. For the slow learner, they are almost foolproof—because every child learns something valuable from such experiences. We realize that taking a class on a trip may be a frightening thought, but we have outlined workable methods and strategies, which make it relatively simple. First you must motivate the children—make them anxious to go because what they will be seeing will interest and intrigue them. Be sure to include them in the choice of specific places, and in planning for the day.

You will find a checklist to help you with the detail work. When

167

you have answered all of the questions, you will have every piece of information you may need in regard to the trip.

If you give your children a specific assignment, consisting of questions they must answer and things they must look for, the trip becomes a truly educational experience; it is also fun, but this is secondary. Give the assignment a day or two before the trip and then have mimeographed copies to hand out as you leave for your destination. The cleverness of your assignment, you will find, will add much to the value of the trip. It should actually be a "class away from school." Encourage any child who wishes to, to bring his camera, and tell him you will be happy to exhibit his photographs. Follow the trip with a full and complete discussion, as well as a review of the answers to the assignment. The things the children have been impressed with may be the basis for writing experience charts, in the lower grades, and for compositions and reports in the upper.

By placing the children in groups, and selecting monitors to take attendance and report back to you, you can structure the situation so that if anyone becomes separated from the group, you will almost immediately be aware of it. Arrange meeting places for anyone who strays to report back to.

Are trips really worthwhile? Absolutely, positively, and most emphatically yes! And for many reasons! They give the children cultural experiences, broaden their backgrounds, and introduce them to new and wonderful things. They break the monotony, enrich the curriculum, and give you a chance to talk with your children, to really communicate and to develop rapport with your slow learners. Aren't these reasons enough?

If you follow the suggestions given, we promise that your group trips will be pleasurable experiences *for you,* and most valuable for the children.

GIVING A CHILD CULTURAL BACKGROUND

The almost complete lack of cultural background, a malady from which so many of our slow learners suffer, is a characteristic of which many teachers are unaware. Most teachers grew up in homes where their parents took them to a variety of different places, introduced them to movies, plays, museums, concerts and the like. With the economically disadvantaged child, so often the slow learner, this is simply not true. There are children who never stray from their own neighborhoods; sometimes their teachers can encourage them to explore, to leave the confines of their "block," and to "see the world." Teachers must realize this —must become aware of the cultural deficiencies, and consequently make an effort to diminish or eliminate them. We must teach our children that "The world is your oyster," and also teach them how to crack it open to get out the meat.

We can illustrate this in no better way than by a story. Two of our young teachers were reading a sign on the Teachers' Bulletin Board: "Hawaii—$449." They were obviously interested as they animatedly discussed it while walking down the hall. A seventh grade boy, walking behind them, said to his friend, "Gee, I ain't never been nowhere." One of the island-bound young ladies turned to him quickly and said, "I can't take you to Hawaii, but have you ever been to Radio City Music Hall?"

"Naw," the youngster replied. He had spent his entire life less than five miles away!

The trip was taken, and was eminently successful.

What did a trip to a theatre bring to this child? It brought to him a new awareness of beauty, of color, of sound. It brought to him a world he never knew existed. It brought to him pleasure and joy. He saw one of the attractions which bring millions of people to his home city, and he heard a full orchestra for the first time in his life.

All of us seem to require some sort of change of environment in our lives. It rejuvenates us, makes our routine, work-a-day world seem brighter, more interesting. Wouldn't the same hold true for our students? Particularly our slow and reluctant learners, for whom experiential learning often succeeds where less attractive methods fall short. By taking the children on enjoyable trips, we give them an awareness of the all-important concept that learning can and should be fun.

Think back to your own school days. Do you remember the trips you took? I hesitate to recall the number of years ago that our civics class went on a boat trip around Manhattan Island. The class has long since been forgotten, but the trip hasn't.

Teachers hesitate to take classes on trips, particularly with the students who need them most. They are afraid the pupils will misbehave, will embarrass them, or will get lost. All of these objections can be overcome. Here are some suggestions. Perhaps you will find them helpful with your classes.

MOTIVATION

"How," you think, "can I take a class like *that* on a trip? They can't sit still for five minutes at a time, they're noisy, they sometimes fight. They're impossible."

No doubt they are; but yes, you can take them. Let's see how. The answer is a word which sometimes is overworked, yet one which must be used: "Motivate!" How? By talking trip, trip, trip for days or weeks before "T-Day." By showing the pupils how interesting the experience will be. By telling them you know you can take them, that they will behave in a manner of which you can be proud. By bringing out how important it is that they cooperate. By including them in the planning, and giving them some of the responsibility involved. In extreme cases it may be necessary to leave the extremely disruptive child at home, but remember that, invariably, this is the child who needs the trip most. It is possible to experiment, telling the boys and girls that if this trip is a success, there will be others, but only for those pupils who cooperate. I used this technique so effectively with a class of non-readers that the bus driver asked me, "Lady, what did you do? Spray them with chloroform?" That eighth grade class was almost afraid to breathe out loud. It was my first trip, and I had overdone it. But one learns as one tries, and I have found that we can bring out the best in children if we make the effort. We rely, too, on their pride in the school, and in their desire to please us.

WHERE SHALL WE GO?

Offer your class a variety of places from which they may choose their destination. Be sure they are all stimulating and appropriate to the children's maturity level. Young children enjoy visiting a zoo! Surprisingly, so do older ones—if you present the experience on their level. For example, "We will study the activities of gorillas and monkeys." Observing them is really fascinating. If your stated purpose is mature, there will be few, if any, complaints. It is axiomatic that we never insult the intelligence of any child, particularly the slow learner.

We suggest you and a group of other teachers in your community develop a list of possible places of interest located in or near your area. The following listing is a basis for it, divided into appropriate places related to the various major subjects. Of course you probably will not find every type of place near home, but you will be pleasantly surprised by the number you do.

Any subject area

National Parks.

Trips on neighboring waters—boat rides or ferries.

State or city parks with special attractions.

Department stores offering tours.

Airports.

Colleges and universities.

Naval or submarine bases.

Army installations.

Concert halls.

Museums of all kinds—art, money, sculpture, natural or historical.

Construction sites—buildings, bridges or tunnels.

Local, unique places of interest (Do not assume your children have visited them—usually they haven't.)

Sports stadiums.

Commercial firms.

Ocean liners or freighters.

Places offering panoramic views.

Wax museums.

Locks, barge canals or seaways.

Science

Aquariums.

Planetariums.

Wildlife preserves.

Museums of natural history.

Coal mines.

Electric power plants.

Geologic phenomena (i.e. New Jersey's Palisades).

Hospitals—offering tours.

Zoos.

Botanical gardens.

Weather bureaus.

Atomic power plants.

Water treatment plants.

Steel mills.

Pet shops.

Medical centers.

Rock quarries.

Consumer testing laboratories.

Mathematics

Banks offering tours.

Stock exchanges offering tours.

Stock brokerages offering tours.

Museums exhibiting various types of currencies (usually associated with banks).

Social studies

National historic monuments.

Historic buildings in the area.

The waterfront—piers, docks, streets.

Manufacturing plants offering tours.

Automobile assembly plants.

Police or fire departments.

Courts.

Settlement houses.

Experimental stations—agriculture, animal husbandry, or fish hatcheries.

Traffic control centers (Radar units, for example).

Wholesale produce markets.

Meat slaughtering and packaging plants.

Food processing plants.

Commercial bakeries.

Commercial laundries.

Language arts

Libraries—local and the largest in the community.

Theatres—movie or legitimate.

Radio broadcasting stations.

Television broadcasting stations.

Newspaper or magazine offices.

Make a survey in your locality and state to see if there are any famous historical sites, landmarks, or geological phenomena. The places under consideration should be discussed with the children. Remember, too, that places which interest adults do not necessarily hold that interest for children. For example, we once took a group to Hyde Park. It meant much less to the boys and girls than to the teachers who remembered Franklin D. Roosevelt. One of the best trips we ever took was to an automobile assembly plant. The actual assembly line is fascinating, particularly when the completed car is driven away at the end. However, there was an added guidance feature to this trip—the children could see how unhappy the people working there appeared to be.

Discuss the possibilities with the class. Would they like to visit a planetarium? Or an aquarium? An airport? The actual choice should, preferably, be left to the class.

Include as much in a group trip as you can. Make it as worth-while as if it were a world tour. If more than one place of interest can be visited the same day, do so, by all means. For example, on the day we visited the automobile assembly plant, we were able to include a stop at the original Edison Laboratories in West Orange, New Jersey. There is a great deal to be seen there; among other things, the children saw the movie studio where Edison made *The Great Train Robbery,* the first moving picture ever made. The gentlemen now serving as guides were actually employed by, and worked with, Thomas Alva Edison, and their reminiscenses were wonderful. Our "tour leader" was amazed when the children asked him to autograph their programs.

TRIP INFORMATION

It is important that you check the destination to obtain the following information. If you do not have it, telephone or write for it.

TRIP QUESTIONNAIRE

1. How long does it take to get to your destination?
2. Which means of transportation would be best?
3. Is the trip appropriate for your grade level?
4. What costs are involved? Are reduced or free admissions available?
5. Where can the pupils have lunch? Can they bring it, or must they buy it?
6. How many parents, if any, will you need?
7. Would it be advisable to take several classes—for companionship, or to share expenses?
8. Do you need reservations?
9. What is the best time of year to take the trip? Is there any period when it is not advisable?
10. Will permission to go be granted by your supervisors?
11. Is it within the financial means of the children? If not, are special funds available?
12. Have you visited this place before, or spoken to an adult who has, to ascertain whether the trip is suitable for your particular class?

13. What benefits will the children derive from the trip? What will they actually learn?
14. Will this trip present any problems in controlling the class? How can these problems be solved?
15. What type of assignment would be best, in relation to this trip? (See "Assigning Work," below.)

When each of these details is worked out, the trip should go relatively smoothly. Then comes the planning with the class. The more we know about a place, the more we will get out of a visit there. Isn't this true when we visit London or Paris? Haven't we been hearing of these places for years? Shouldn't students visiting Stratford, Connecticut, know about Stratford-on-Avon as well? Isn't a trip to the Cloisters similar to visiting a church in Spain or Italy? Teach the children the significance of the building and of its art treasures. Spend time working with your slow learners, explaining carefully to them what, specifically, they will see, and why it is important. Relate this to previous knowledge— in other words, tie in the trip with material the child already knew. This will make it truly meaningful.

ASSIGNING WORK

Prepare an assignment for the children to complete when they return from the trip. Give them, in class the day before, a series of questions, the answers to which they will find while sightseeing. Discuss and cover, beforehand, the background information and, if necessary, mimeograph and distribute it. Instruct the children, too, to make note of things which they learned, or which interested them. These devices will make the experience a more vital and meaningful one. Museums are among the most amazing places in the entire world, and yet trips there can be dull, unless the students are going to see specific things, answer questions and really observe. Our work is to make sure they do so.

PICTURE TAKING

Some of the children may have cameras, and would like to take them along. By all means, permit them to do so. The teacher might take his camera too, and work with the slow children, showing them how to use it. His manner should be warm and encouraging. This will do much to prevent discipline problems during the trip.

Teaching an incidental lesson like the use of a camera might throw open doors to learning and to creativity that may otherwise have been forever shut to the children. I have a friend who was labeled a slow learner for many years. He suffered from severe attacks of asthma. Concentration upon his school work was consequently very difficult for him—he became hostile and extremely unwilling to learn or even attend school. A perceptive teacher noticed that the child, who seemed to be very sensitive, took a profound interest in pictures. "They tell stories," he would say.

One afternoon, on a field trip with the class, the teacher taught the reluctant learner how to use a camera. Today this child is an accomplished photographer. This teacher has always boasted that she taught children, not subjects.

An interesting exhibit may be made of photographs taken on a trip. If you notify your children beforehand, they may be motivated by this fact to bring their cameras.

FOLLOW-UP LESSONS

If the trip is not followed by a discussion and a follow-up assignment, it loses some of its value. Nor is, "Why did you find this trip interesting?" adequate. Challenge the children. Make them think about what they saw. If they were impressed, how can you get them to tell you about it—or to show you? A critique is good. The students can discuss the pros and cons of the places of interest, tell you how the trip can be improved. Ask, too, about surprising discoveries which they may have encountered. I shall never forget the thirteen year old girl who came up to me and said, after a trip to a planetarium, "But I thought the moon was made of cheese!"

Have the slow learner write a summary of his reactions and ask him to review for you what he learned as a result of the trip. This might be used in the class or school newspaper. By doing this kind of assignment, he is forced to think and he benefits, too, by the physical act of writing.

AVOIDING LOSSES

There are many ways of physically setting up the trip so that it is as easy as possible for you, the teacher. One method which has proved successful is to divide the class into groups of five or six pupils. These may be made up of friends, a procedure which young people like, or by calling off names alphabetically. Each unit of five or six is one group. Prepare your lists beforehand. Within the group one person, the sergeant-at-arms, is chosen whose function is to report to the teacher whenever a "head check" is necessary. This is done at least seven or eight times during the day—before leaving, upon assembling at the destination, while touring, and when leaving for home. It takes one minute, when done in this manner, and it saves the teacher endless countings.

As added insurance, we have found that if the area to be covered is a large one, it is good to select a "rendezvous point." This is a central location, to which anyone can go if he becomes separated from the class. A teacher or other adult will return to this spot if anyone is missing. We did this when we took 500 pupils to the World's Fair (New York, 1965). It worked very well. Only one boy strayed—he'd won a prize at one of the pavilions, and had stayed behind to claim it. He couldn't find his group— who, incidentally, should have waited for him. But he went to the rendezvous point and there we found him. Emphasize to your children the necessity for staying together, make frequent head checks, and you can actually relax and enjoy yourself.

How to travel? If public transportation is available, it is usually the most inexpensive way to travel. There are times when renting a bus is preferable, and relatively easy. All arrangements can be made by telephone, and we have found the bus companies to be very cooperative.

VALUE OF TRIPS

Any trip has its problems, big or small. It is extra work for the teacher, and requires extra expenditures of energy. Why go? What values accrue? Let us see:

We must broaden the horizons for all of the children we teach, particularly the slow learners. There are a great many people who live and die within a small radius of their homes. We have it within our power to show them that there is more to the world than exists in their own backyards. Hopefully, they will then seek it. Children will often see things on class trips they have never seen before. Surely this is an important part of education.

Slow learners love trips. They are something to look forward to, to break the monotony of everyday school. They are a chance to spread wings, and move out into the world. Is it not criminal for a child to grow up in New York City and never see a play with real-live actors, in a theatre? Watch the way pupils behave just before a trip. The air of anticipation, the conversation, the attitudes are all related to it. For many children, this is really traveling. Talk about the trip, build up enthusiasm and make it as exciting as you can. This is easy if you have already visited the place, but even if you haven't, it can still be done. Speak to someone who can give you details, and then discuss some, but not all, of the things the class will see. Whet their appetites. Treat the boys and girls as if they are mature young people, who know how to handle themselves in all situations. Give them the opportunity to meet the challenge.

Adolescents today are constantly seeking new experiences. Their rock and roll music and psychedelic art are examples of this. Let us give them experiences that are interesting but wholesome. Let us show them that adults are not stuffed shirts, that we, too, are seeking to expand our minds and our lives. Seeing an electric eel give off currents of electricity is thrilling. So is seeing a play like *Man of La Mancha*. These are the kinds of experiences we, as teachers, should and can introduce.

We cannot neglect the use of trips as a device for teaching the slow learner, particularly because the impressions made are lasting ones. When tied in with the curriculum, this is even truer. A natural history museum is the best place in the world for teaching the concept of life as it existed in prehistoric times. If you have ever doubted it, visit the dinosaur halls, and study the fossils. Can you picture how graphic this is—how long children will remember it? Rarely can we find teaching tools which are so impressive. After reading Julius Caesar, shouldn't the pupils see it performed? If a class is studying French, shouldn't they have a chance to hear it spoken in a film? The experiences you can give them are endless.

Another bonus a trip can offer is a chance to communicate with the slow learner in a relaxed, adult situation. You may find some boys or girls very anxious to sit and talk with you—to exchange ideas about things other than subject matter. If a teacher can develop rapport with the children, teaching in the classroom becomes even easier, and trips are a great help in doing this.

By seeking out troubled children and really talking with them (not, by the way, to them), you may be able to find ways to get together, to get them to learn during the hours they spend in your class. Very often you will find they are troubled as well as troublesome. A child who bursts out in school may be constantly the butt at home. A girl who screams epithets at a male teacher may actually be shouting them at her absent father. You may be able to learn more about a child and his problems on a bus trip than during the many hours you spend with him in the classroom. This, too, may make the entire trip worthwhile.

Education is a many faceted thing. We learn by use of our senses—and far too often through the eyes alone. We try to have children read textbooks, but for the slow learner, textbooks are one facet, and not a particularly shining one at that. Should we not strive for facets which will attract attention, cultivate knowledge, and remain with the children throughout their lives? Such a one is the experiential. Experiences are the jewels the children will carry away from the school. You, the teacher, are in a position to dispense these jewels; and, in this context, trips are "diamonds." And they are diamonds for children of all ages.

Older children may appear unaffected by these experiences because they are trying to project another kind of image. They are "playing it cool." Actually, they can and do become involved and interested, if we are successful in our teaching! Before they leave us, it is important that we give to them lasting impressions of the things we have found which interest us. We can, of course, merely introduce them—let them glimpse the facets. At least, though, we are making the young people aware of the existence of museums, of theatres, of historical places, of the unusual and of the interesting. We can help to graphically unfold for them the fascination of the thousands of years of history of mankind.

How many trips should a class take during a school year? For the slow learner, the more frequent they are, the better; honestly, we believe that one trip every two weeks is not excessive. However, this is, of course, up to you the teacher. If you find trips are valuable, and not too enervating for you, we are sure you will experiment more and more in this area.

SUMMARY

In this chapter we have tried to convince you of the value of taking your class on frequent trips, and have tried to show why it is particularly important to give your slow learners new, interesting experiences. As teachers we must help to build up within these children positive feelings toward cultural experiences; we can do this by taking them to places which will intrigue them, which they will enjoy.

In order to have a successful trip, it is necessary for you to motivate the children—to make them enthusiastic and cooperative. You are able to do this if you involve them in the choice of destination, and in planning for the entire day. Offer a number of suggestions so that they are really selecting, not accepting your choice. We have included a listing of many types of places which are of interest to slow learners.

Have the class help you with the detail work by answering, with you, the ten questions in a Trip Questionnaire. Prepare an assignment, and give it to the children in the classroom, the day before the trip. If there is a need for background material, be sure you give them that in advance, as well.

Encourage the children to take their cameras with them, and, if you are able to do so, assist them with their photography. To avoid constantly "counting heads," assign your children to small groups, and have one monitor from each report to you when you request a check.

Just as traveling abroad is of educational value, so is traveling in one's own area. For some of your slow learners, these may easily be the most distant trips they will take. For others, these class excursions will serve as introductions to a new and far wider world. You will discover, too, that you have greater opportunities to communicate with your children and develop rapport with them. As is true in every aspect of teaching, motivation, planning, ingenuity, and creativity will pay big dividends in connection with group trips. You can insure the success of such endeavors if you make full use of each of these characteristics, and you need feel no anxiety, for your children will appreciate the opportunities you are giving them.

These trips can be the magic carpet that transports our slow learners from their hum-drum, everyday life, to places lit with wonder and delight. We have observed that intellectual familiarity does not breed contempt. On the contrary, it quickens our sympathies for people of other places and other creeds and colors, helping to unite us in understanding and love for one another.

11

developing tests for the slow learner

Before a physician can cure an illness, he must make a careful and accurate diagnosis of the case. This is often done by having various tests performed in the medical laboratory. We, too, have illnesses to cure, diagnoses to make and consequently must do careful testing. A variety of tests are at our disposal. First let us consider the standardized tests; the printed tests we use most frequently to determine the children's progress in reading and mathematics. They compare the children with others in the same age group and grade. However, they do not take into consideration the child's background, his environment and his creative talents. They are valuable for diagnosis, for they aid us in determining wherein the child's specific problems lie. They are, however, only one of the tools we have, and their importance should not be over-emphasized.

Teacher-made tests are far more valuable if they are well constructed, because they give us information in regard to the material or skills the children have not mastered. Every test taken by the slow learner should be analyzed by the teacher if it is to be of maximum value, for this will help to determine the particular needs of the slow learner. Tests also give the youngsters an estimation of their own capabilities, and they see wherein their own problem areas lie.

In another vein, tests may be used to stimulate the children's thinking if the questions are skillful and interesting. You are able to emphasize the most important points, concepts and ideas of the work you have been teaching, by including them in your tests.

There are many types of questions you may use: true-false,

completion, multiple choice, matching, interpreting diagrams or graphs, and then actually drawing them. The slow learner must be taught the techniques for answering essay and thought questions. We suggest a method for marking papers which will motivate the children, and cut down markedly on your work. Also included is a method for building a success pattern through testing.

Where children have difficulty reading, we ask you to consider giving them individual, oral tests. They also need practice in writing answers, for without this practice they cannot succeed in future academic work. Children may also write questions for your examinations, which they enjoy, and from which they learn a great deal. You may wish to try open book tests, on occasion, to vary the routine. Above all, we want to emphasize the idea that tests should be given at the end of a unit of work, and not religiously each week, or every two weeks. They should be used to diagnose, to review and to reiterate—but never to keep children busy or to punish them. They should never be used to stigmatize children, but rather as an incentive to acquire knowledge.

USING TESTS FOR DIAGNOSIS

In developing our tests we must be aware, and take into consideration, the intellectual level of the slow learner, so that he does not "block," and so that he does not become discouraged. There are many arguments against tests—the fact that some people freeze up and can't do well on them, the fact that the results are often invalid, the fact that they take much time and effort on the part of the teachers, time and effort better spent teaching. But we are here to discuss the "pros," the case *for* tests—the fact that they do have value, and can prove to be an excellent tool for teaching the slow learner when used wisely. However, let us stress the word "wisely," for that is the key.

First, let us differentiate between standardized tests and those which are teacher-made. Almost every one of us has taken many of both types. Let us review the differences. Standardized tests are the printed tests we use most frequently in such areas as reading and mathematics. They are so named because they have been given to a very large number of children, and, using the results of the testing, have been changed and worked on so that they are the product of much experimentation, much variation and correction. Questions which proved either too simple or too difficult have been eliminated, and the resulting examination is supposed to give a good indication of the child's ability in the specific area—compared with the abilities of the huge number of other children who were tested. Intelligence tests fall into this category.

It has been found, however, that these tests are often inaccurate, because they rely on the cultural background of the child —an intellectual or educational background he may, through no fault of his own, lack. Such backgrounds, however, are often taken for granted—and this is particularly true in the case of standardized testing.

There are a large number of such standardized tests, and their value lies in judicious use. We cannot compare the proverbial silk purse with a sow's ear. Nor can we compare the achievements of all children—living anywhere in the world, and with different cultural and socio-economic backgrounds. Within your class, however, the results of these tests may be used to indicate the directions your teaching must take—because they will disclose the skills and knowledges your children are lacking—the holes in your boys' and girls' education.

Very often the results of the standardized tests in reading and in mathematics are given in terms of "Grade Level." We will say, "Mary Jane is reading one year below grade level." What do we actually mean? We are saying Mary Jane's results on the particular test are equal to those of the large majority of pupils in the grade one year below hers. If Mary Jane is in grade 7, her results are equal to those of the majority of pupils in grade 6.

Standardized tests are valuable when they are considered as only one tool at the teacher's disposal. The results are often used by administrators to establish classes, and to determine the child's level of achievement. They may be, however, misleading, when considered without reviewing the child's achievements in his class work, and his previous grades. In no way do standardized tests give any indication of the children's creative abilities.

Since reading tests usually consider two particular aspects, vocabulary knowledge and comprehension, we may study the results of the tests to determine which skills the child needs to learn, and supply appropriate work and assistance. The same is true of the mathematics examinations. Because they are divided into various areas, the teacher is able to use the results to learn which skills he must teach—to the entire class or to the individual child. Billy can't do fractions, while Patty doesn't understand problems of area. When used in this way, the tests have far more value than if we look at the results and say, "Too bad, Billy is below grade level in math." The tests can be used as a barometer of the children's needs.

HOW CAN TESTS BE OF VALUE?

Mommy, do I have to go to school today?
Of course, dear. Why? Is something bothering you?
My stomach hurts. It hurts a lot.
But, darling, you almost always feel sick on Fridays. What happens in school on Friday?
That's the day we get our spelling test. I feel so sick.

What makes this little soap-opera vignette so sad are two facts: One, it's true! Two, the little girl is in the second grade!

What are we doing to our children? Are we taking the joy out of learning and making it a source of frustration, of tension, or pressure, of ulcers? It has been said, "We teach as we have been taught—not as we have been taught to teach." Are we carrying forth a tradition of rigidity, of dull rote learning betraying a total lack of creativity? A test every Friday is dull, ineffective, and unnecessary.

Suit your testing to your teaching. You will surely need to do some testing, but adjust it to the material you are covering and, even more so, to the slow children you are teaching.

1. Construct your tests so that they give you a very good idea of which content and skills your children have mastered, and which need reteaching, for it's not impossible to find many pupils within a class who did not grasp the work you have covered.

When you give a test, analyze the results. Which questions did the children miss? Was it all of the class, the majority, or simply the slow learners? If it was the majority of the class, you may wish to reteach the work to everyone. If it is a smaller number, you may decide to divide the class into groups, and teach only those children who need the additional help in this specific area. The others may be given enrichment material at this time.

Your tests should reveal the weaknesses the slow learners have. You may wish to work with these children, individually. While the entire class is working, you may sit down with the child, teach him what he needs to learn and then assign homework reviewing the material. When he brings that in, you would check it to be sure the child has mastered it. For example, there are children who constantly write run-on sentences. You may work with them on this, then give them mimeographed material to correct. Here is a paragraph you might distribute to children who have just had a lesson on this subject:

> Our class was asked by our teacher to write a paragraph about our favorite television programs which we watch either daily, weekly, Sundays or on special occasions. I like to watch Batman, my sister—My Three Sons, my brother—Bonanza and my father—always turns on the news because he says we should be aware of what is going on in the world. We watch it too because he says so but I don't like it it's so boring to just see the war; my mother thinks so too. When I have my own television set I'll watch the late show, I'll watch the late late show, I'll watch the late, late, late show.

2. If you give tests at the end of a unit of work, both you and your children will be able to tell whether or not they have mastered this unit of work, or if they need more work on a particular subject. It is to give them this awareness that the test has value.

3. You can, by use of tests, stimulate the children's thinking. If your questions are skillful and interesting, your children will respond to the stimulation. For example, any of these questions might motivate children:

> *a.* Ben Franklin's *Poor Richard's Almanac* is often quoted. What did he mean when he said, "Small strokes fell great oaks"?

b. Our national motto is "E pluribus unum." Why was it chosen?

c. We often hear quotations from the Bible. What is meant by this one, "I will not by evil be ever dismayed."

d. Each morning in many schools pupils recite the "Pledge of Allegiance." What is allegiance, and why do we owe it to our flag?

4. It is often great fun to inject special questions, ringers into tests. For example,

a. If a plane crashed on the border between the U.S. and Mexico, where would the survivors be buried?

b. Brothers and sisters I have none, but that man's father is my father's son. Who am I?

c. How will it be possible for a person to leave New York at 3 P.M. and arrive in Los Angeles at 2 P.M.—in other words to get there before he left? (Clue: when the trip takes less than three hours, and this is in the very near future, this will be true. There is a three hour time difference between the east and the west coasts, and when the trip takes two hours, you will arrive earlier than you leave. If you leave New York at noon, it is 9 A.M. in Los Angeles. Two hours later, it is 2 P.M. in New York, 11 A.M. in Los Angeles.)

These questions have value, in addition to being fun. They, too, stimulate the children to think. Don't be afraid to use them— but one at a time, and not on every test. On a long test, particularly of the objective, short answer variety, the children react well to the change of pace this offers them.

5. A test may serve as a graphic summary to help "nail down" certain ideas and concepts for your slow learners.

By your choice of questions, you show which material is most important, and which is of lesser import. If, however, you stress trivia, you defeat this purpose. Certainly your essay questions should be of the material which you feel is most significant. You do not try to "trip up" your children. Your test is still a teaching tool, a way of repeating, reiterating, rephrasing and restressing what you have already covered.

TEACHER-MADE AND PUPIL-MADE TESTS

The customary teacher-made test may consist of various types of questions which are excellent for the slow learner.

1. True-False.

   The pupil indicates whether a statement is true or false:

   a. The lead ship in Columbus' group was the Pinta.

   b. An adverb modifies a noun or pronoun.

   c. The reciprocal of ⅓ is 3.

2. A variation of this type of question is to correct a false statement, making it true.

   The lead ship in Columbus' group was the Santa Maria.

   An adverb modifies a verb, adjective or another verb.

   The reciprocal of ⅓ is 3. True.

3. Completion: The pupil fills in the missing word.

   a. The President of the U.S. during the time of the Louisiana Purchase was _____.

   b. $e=mc^2$ is the formula developed by _____.

4. Multiple Choice: The student must select the correct answer:

   (*a*) The nation with the largest population in the world today is: (*a*) U.S.   (*b*) Argentina   (*c*) India   (*d*) Russia   (*e*) China

   (*b*) The correct square root of 625 is: (*a*) 15   (*b*) 20   (*c*) 30   (*d*) 40   (*e*) none of these

   (*c*) The following characters are from the works of Charles Dickens: (*a*) Tiny Tim   (*b*) Stryver   (*c*) Mr. Macawber   (*d*) none of these   (*e*) all of these

5. Matching questions:

Two columns of terms are listed. The pupil must relate one with the other.

a.	Van Gogh	1.	Portrait in Greys and Blacks
b.	Picasso	2.	The Night Watch
c.	Whistler	3.	La Guernica
d.	Gainsborough	4.	The Potato Eaters
e.	Rembrandt	5.	The Blue Boy

Very often the number of items doesn't coincide—so that one column is longer than the other, and one or two items are not matched.

6. Diagram or graphs.

The pupil is asked to:

Draw and label a diagram of the eye.

Draw a graph to show the population growth in New York in the last fifty years.

7. Interpret a diagram or graph:

Label it.

Interpret the graph in Illustration 11-1, in terms of annual income and years of education.

ESSAYS

The slow learner must be trained in the technique of answering thought questions and essays. It is a good idea to work individually with each slow child. Throughout his school career, and also in his later life when he is seeking employment, he will be confronted with such questions. We do him a grave injustice if we do not train him to answer them.

Emphasize the following points:

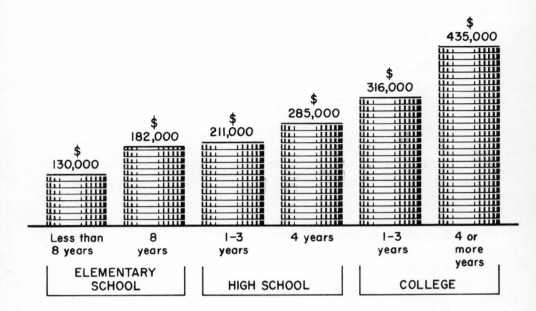

Illustration 11-1

1. Analyze the question—what is asked for?

2. What is the logical answer? Why?

3. After he writes his response, train him to reread it, and ask himself, "Has the question been carefully answered? Have I given the information asked for in the question?"

4. Have I given enough information? Very often, the slow learner does not.

8. Thought questions.

A thought question requires one or several sentences to answer it. It may be a how or a why question:

How did Harriet Beecher Stowe earn the remark, attributed to Abraham Lincoln, "So you are the little lady who started this war."?

9. Essay questions:

A good essay question certainly is thought provoking, and requires as its answer a body of related information.

> What were the factors which brought about Hitler's rise to power?
>
> Of what value is our space program?
>
> Why is the population growing at such a rate that it is referred to as the "population explosion"? What effects will this have on the world's food supply?

Never give a test, grade it, and put the marks into your record book. You lose most of the value of the test. Rather than that, have the children grade it, review the grades, have the pupils determine which areas they need to be retaught, and assign as homework correct completion of the questions on the test. It is the worst pedagogy possible to give a test and never return it to the student. It is almost as bad to just give him a grade, without allowing him to see the paper. Tests are teaching tools, and should be used as such.

GRADING TESTS

It is possible to cut down on your work a great deal by having your students grade their own papers. To do this effectively, we have found the following system extremely good. It motivates

X	A	D	R	S
X	A	D	R	S
X	A	D	R	S
X	A	D	R	S
X	A	D	R	S

Illustration 11-2

pupils, makes the process of marking exciting, and stimulates discussion and expression.

1. After the test is finished, collect the papers by rows (Illustration 11-2).

Give the papers of row X to row D. Change papers in the following order:

Row D to row S; Row S to Row A; Row A to row R; Row R to X.

Row D now has the papers of row X.
Row S now has the papers of row D.
Row A now has the papers of row S.
Row R now has the papers of row A.
Row X now has the papers of Row R.

In other words, the first row exchanges papers with the third. The third row gives its papers to the fifth. The fifth gives its papers to the second, and the second to the fourth.

You may use any variation of this, but do not have neighbors correcting each other's work. If you have had the pupils write in ink, then have them correct in pencil, or vice-versa.

At the top of each page, have the pupil correcting the paper write: "Corrected by" and sign his name. He thereby has the responsibility for that particular paper.

2. Assign point values to each answer. Try to have these simple—no half points, for example:

Instruct the pupils: If an answer is correct, do not put any mark on it. If it is wrong, indicate the amount of credit to be deducted by writing —5, —3 or whatever value the question has. A short quiz might look like Illustration 11-3.

3. Add the deductions and circle the total.

If the entire examination were short answers, this total is deducted from 100, and the grade placed on the top of the paper. When there is an essay question, it is suggested that the teacher mark it, although it is possible and profitable for the pupils to do so. It is more complicated, however. You must outline what points must be in the essay for it to get full credit, and how much each of these is worth.

4. After the papers have been marked, return them to the

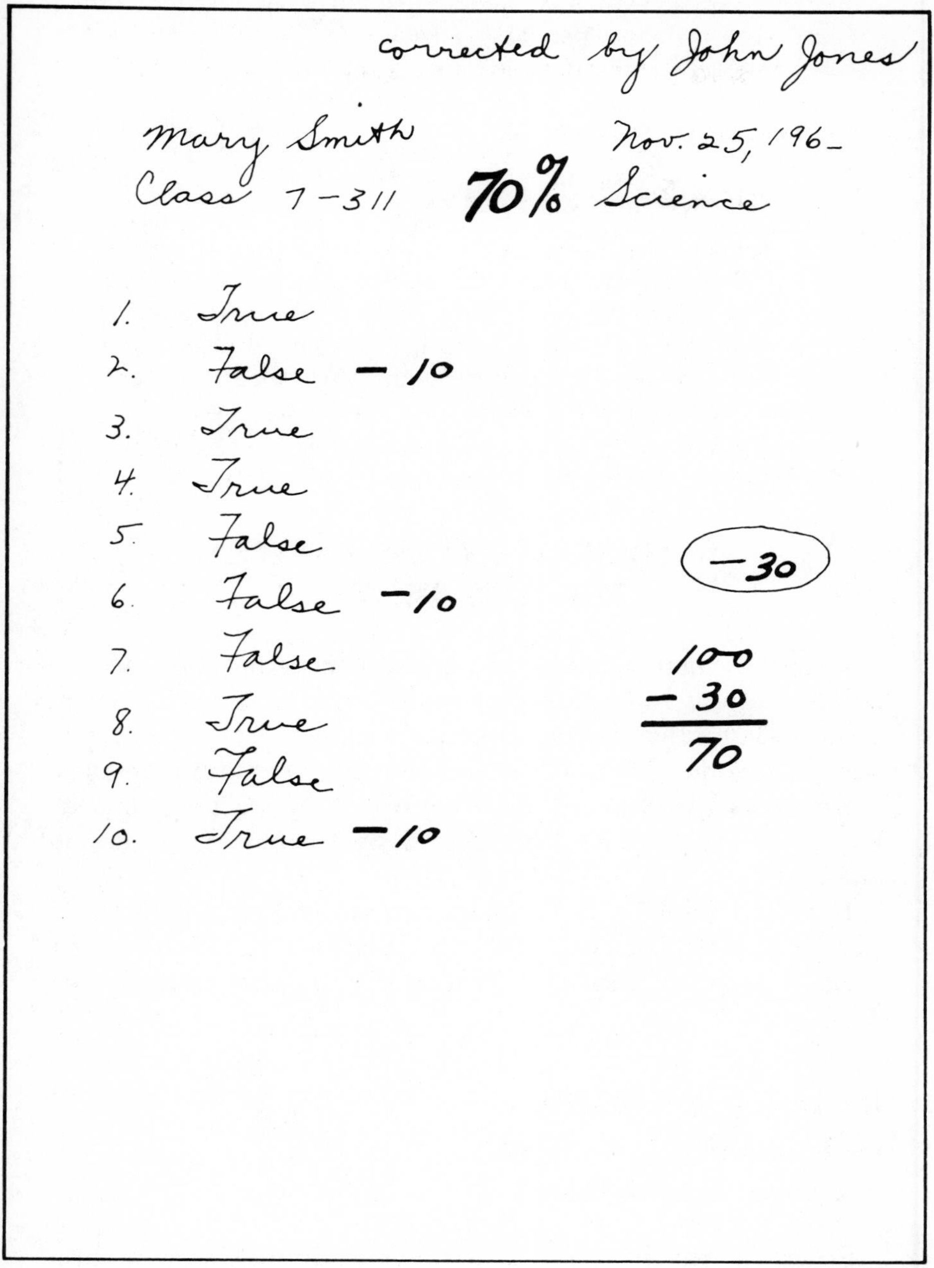

corrected by John Jones

Mary Smith   Nov. 25, 196_
Class 7-311   **70%** Science

1. True
2. False — 10
3. True
4. True
5. False
6. False —10   (—30)
7. False
8. True   100
9. False   — 30
10. True —10   70

Illustration 11-3

owners for final checking. This is when the action occurs. You may give part credit, if you wish. A pupil will say, I have "such and such on my paper. May I have some credit for it?" It becomes a game, but an interesting one. Make sure the pupils check the arithmetic, the addition of the points lost, and their correct subtraction from 100.

5. The value of this method lies in several areas.

a. In correcting the papers, you repeat the correct answers twice. You thereby reinforce the learning experience, and you save a lot of time by having your pupils do the correcting.

b. You stimulate active participation. The students, you will find, will fight for a single point. We called it "finding points," and most of them tried very hard to find even one.

c. Even the slow learners are fully capable of handling this if the marking progresses slowly.

BUILDING A SUCCESS PATTERN
THROUGH TESTING

There are many children who begin their pattern of academic failure early in their lives, and never seem to recover from it. Success eludes them as the sun on a rainy day. Yet as the sun is there, above the clouds, so too should success be waiting to come out. How can we bring it out? One way is by teaching children how to study. Another is by ingeniously teaching them how to take tests.

If you are teaching slow children, or any youngsters who need additional help (because, until now, they have tasted few of the fruits of success), there are a number of possible methods you may try:

Be sure your children understand the material you have taught them

Determine this by questions, by review, by rephrasing and repeating the most important concepts—and by discussing them.

Give your children rexographed or mimeographed information for them to study

Do not make it too complicated, too overwhelming. Be concrete, as specific as you can be.

For example, in handling a relatively difficult concept—the structure of matter—one might hand out this review sheet:

Matter

1. What is *matter*?

Scientists say *matter* is anything which takes up space and has weight.

The entire universe, and everything in it is made up of matter—stone, wood, plants, animals, even the air we breathe is made of matter.

2. What is the smallest part of matter?

We call the smallest particles of matter *molecules*. There are molecules of stone, or wood, skin or leaf, gold or copper, of oxygen. We cannot see these particles without the aid of a very powerful microscope because they are so small.

3. What moves matter?

When matter moves, there must be *energy* to move it. When you walk, when the wind blows, when water boils, energy is needed. Energy is force, and we cannot see it, but we see its effects.

QUESTIONS

1. A piece of cotton has _____ in it.
2. To move that piece of cotton requires _____.
3. Our bodies are made of _____.
4. Which is correct?
    a. A molecule is made of matter? Yes_____ No_____
    b. Matter is made up of molecules? Yes_____ No_____

    c. Both Yes_____ No_____

    d. Water is a form of energy or matter? _____

  5. What do you know about molecules which proves they are very small?

  6. You know matter takes up space, and _____
_____.

Should most pupils be able to answer these questions (seventh grade science)? Aren't they simple enough to help build a success pattern? The teacher would have to try them to determine this. But once, having learned the children's level, he should work at or below it, to help them to see that they can learn, they can succeed. Remember, such a sheet as the one outlined above is used for review purposes only.

Then, when giving a test, he would ask such questions as:

> What takes up space and has weight?
> What is the smallest amount of water possible?
> What do we call a force which moves matter?

What we are doing here is asking for exactly the information we have fed the pupils. Why? To help them to see that they can learn, they can succeed; to build up their self-confidence. Skillful questioning is one ingenious means of review. A test can constitute the résumé of a month's work. Incidentally, as a résumé of a unit of work, the children might compose the questions for the test.

Give oral tests

Pupils who have difficulty reading do not necessarily have difficulty with subject matter. It will often surprise you when you see this. They can answer questions, if they do not have to read them. Once they have to read they are defeated.

If you wish to test such students, why not read the questions aloud? With slower classes, try for, but do not demand, perfect spelling.

It is true—reading questions aloud obviously helps to ignore the fundamental problem, but it also lets you test the subject you are teaching, rather than the reading.

You may choose to give personalized tests. Call your students up to the desk, and question each, individually. This can only be successful if the rest of the class is gainfully employed, and is useless under other conditions. But, using this method, you are able to vary your testing to fit the needs of your children and to assist them in the technique of answering questions. For example, if a child defines the word "composition" by the expression "to make," you point out that the word "composition" is a noun, and that we define a noun with another noun, never by a verb, so the correct definition would be "something that is made." As we have said, even within the group you will find much variation. The important thing is that you are interested in helping the child to feel that he is not "stupid," that he can succeed in academic work. You help nourish his self-esteem which may have been damaged by repeated failure. What is more important?

Have them write!

All children, and especially the slow learner, need to do a great deal of writing. They need to learn the skill of putting words together. On each written test you give, have one question which must be answered in a sentence or two. In homework assignments, start the children writing—perhaps utilizing such leading statements as: "I think molecules are very small because _____

_____."

Children who rarely write almost forget how. Even asking them for long, oral answers helps them in the development of their communication skills, which so many of them need. For people who have no problems expressing themselves—and surely most teachers fall into this group—it is hard to empathize, to feel the way a child feels who has trouble putting his thoughts into words. But we must emphathize, we are to teach "the whole child" rather than merely our own subject.

To train a child to write answers to questions, first ask him questions which require long verbal answers. Then casually while working with him individually, hand him his pencil, and in an informal, friendly way tell him, "Now let's write these answers down, so that you can finish your test."

To teach children to write, the same procedure may be followed. Discuss the topic with them, drawing from them their ideas, verbally, whenever possible. If the ideas are good, praise them at every opportunity. Contribute a few thoughts yourself, to further stimulate their thinking. Then have them put down on paper the ideas which you discussed together, saying, "If we found these ideas interesting, someone reading them will also find them worthwhile."

When children make requests of you, have them put the desired favor in the form of a friendly letter. Do the same when they wish to communicate with anyone else in the school—for example, they might sometimes wish to invite the principal or another teacher to a class party.

You might also have them write letters to sick classmates or friends.

The copying of notes from the board, the answering of written questions, and even the old-fashioned method of copying model letters will tend to make a child more comfortable when he picks up his pen.

All of these devices will help the child to answer test questions with greater facility.

Writing their own questions

It often proves interesting to have children write their own questions, and submit them to you. You select from these to make up your test. It's fun—using the children's words. You will find they will use your style—almost exactly. Many times more than one child will submit the same questions—and you may comment with a smile, to them, "Great minds with but a single thought." Youngsters get a "kick" out of recognizing their work, and, if they miss the question, it becomes hilarious—providing it doesn't happen too often.

Open book tests

In our colleges, open book tests are given frequently. On our level it should be the same genus, but a far simpler species. Give questions the answers to which the children can find without being excellent readers. Use the novelty of the situation, and give additional help to those who particularly need it.

Parental signatures

Because parents so frequently complain that they are not aware of their children's weekly progress, we suggest you have at least one test paper per month signed and returned to you. Leave room for the signature, and for parental remarks. If you have any comments, write them on the paper, immediately above the place for the parent's signature.

For example, at the end of a mimeographed test, you may use this form:

Date_____	_____
	Parent's signature
_____	_____
Teacher's comments	Parent's comments

In this way the test becomes a means of communication between you and the parent—which is absolutely essential in the case of the slow learner.

SUMMARY

Our prime purpose, so often, for giving tests is that we may assign a grade to every student. However, we have tried to show the many other ways in which they may be used in your teaching —to diagnose, to review, to stimulate, to motivate, to build a success pattern, and to communicate with parents. They are tools well worth using.

CONCLUSION

In writing of the methods we have used, or seen used success-fully to teach the slow learner, we have first tried to help you recognize him and be aware of his problems. We have suggested techniques to plan lessons, in terms of yearly and daily work. We have outlined procedures for wholesome discipline, and given many methods to be utilized in each subject area. Because it is so important, that you gain the cooperation of the parents, we have explained our ways of accomplishing this. We've attempted to list procedures to make trips simple and pleasant. Testing, too, is discussed with strategies which we hope you will enjoy adopting.

Above all, we want to leave you with these thoughts: Let us use every wholesome and salutary influence to foster in our slow learners a love of learning—a teacher's charm, his warmth, his whole-hearted interest and understanding of the child, his peda-gogical powers, his smile—these are his weapons to fight ignorance and its far-reaching disasters.

index